A Brief History of Tassajara

From Native American Sweat Lodges
to Pioneering Zen Monastery

Marilyn McDonald

Cuke Press
PO Box 151471, San Rafael, CA 94915
www.cuke.com/cuke-press
cuke-press@cuke.com

A Brief History of Tassajara:
from Native American Sweat Lodges to Pioneering Zen Monastery
by Marilyn McDonald
Foreword by David Chadwick

Copyright © 2018 Marilyn McDonald
Foreword & Afterword copyright © 2018 David Chadwick
All rights reserved.
First edition: 2018

Publisher's Cataloging-In-Publication Data
(Prepared by The Donohue Group, Inc.)

Names: McDonald, Marilyn, 1940-2017. | Chadwick, David, 1945- writer of supplementary textual content.
Title: A brief history of Tassajara : from Native American sweat lodges to pioneering Zen monastery / Marilyn McDonald ; [foreword by David Chadwick].
Description: First edition. | San Rafael, CA : Cuke Press, 2018. | Includes bibliographical references and index.
Identifiers: ISBN 9781732287709
Subjects: LCSH: Tassajara Zen Mountain Center—History. | Zen monasteries—California—History. | Sweatbaths—California—History. | Hot springs—California—History. | Ventana Wilderness (Calif.)—History. | BISAC: HISTORY / United States / State & Local / West. | TRAVEL / United States / West / Pacific. | RELIGION / Buddhism / Zen.
Classification: LCC BQ6377.C22 T37 2018 | DDC 294.3/9270979476—dc23

Library of Congress Control Number: 2018945607

ISBN-13: 978-1-7322877-0-9

Cover design by Lawrence Burns

Front and back cover photos used with permission from
Mayo Hayes O'Donnell Library

This book contains photos and clippings collected by Marilyn McDonald in the nineteen seventies and eighties. If permission is lacking for an item, please notify us via the Cuke Press address above.

10 9 8 7 6 5 4 3

Dedicated to the memory of Marilyn McDonald.

CONTENTS

Foreword vii

Introduction xi

Native Americans at Tassajara 1

Tassajara Hot Springs Resort 5

Tassajara Zen Center 131

Afterword 145

Appendix 149

McDonald's Acknowledgements 170

On Producing this Book 171

Author photo 174

Index 175

FOREWORD

DURING THE TASSAJARA Zen Mountain Center guest season of 1974, I had the position of head monk, really more of a head student, which allowed me plenty of time to relate to guests as well as other students. I'd run the guest dining room for the first four summers and was accustomed to being with guests. One repeat visitor I was pleased to see that guest season was Jack Novcich. I went over to the dining room toward the end of the meal to say hello to that great old character. That's when I met a new arrival, Marilyn Doyle, who later became Marilyn McDonald. She was sitting across from Jack and was obviously fascinated with a story he was telling about the old days. Marilyn was friendly and curious. She had an immediate interest in the history of the place and, fortunately for her, dear old Jack Novcich was there to talk to her at any length she wished about what he'd seen and heard in the sixty years or so he'd been coming. I saw her and Jack together a lot during her stay. She tells about meeting him in the introduction and he's quoted a few times in this book, the culmination of the years of in-depth investigation that Marilyn embarked on that day.

I got to share some highlights of Marilyn's progress the next year when I was director. By then she knew more about Tassajara history than anyone I knew except Jack. I admired her for sticking with it, and felt we were kindred spirits in that I was focused then in my free time on studying Zen writings and chants in the original. I saw in Marilyn that same sort of drive and suggested that maybe we had the research gene.

After that year I didn't live at Tassajara but returned for short stays in the summer and sometimes would be there when she was, her store of knowledge about Tassajara's past ever vaster. I lost track of Marilyn but would think of her when I'd pick up the scrapbook she'd left us with historical clippings, photos, and stories.

In the late 1980s I got into writing about my experiences in Japan and Zen Center and about the life, teaching, and community of the San Francisco Zen Center's founder, Shunryu Suzuki. A few websites grew out of that work. One, cuke.com, included interviews and background. Early last year I decided to create a page for pre–Zen Center Tassajara history to gather in one place what there was here and there on the site and elsewhere within easy reach. I remembered Marilyn and her work and decided to contact her. I sent a message to Leslie James, a senior teacher in Zen Center, who along with her husband Keith Meyerhoff has been living at Tassajara and Tassajara's way station at Jamesburg for many years. I learned then that Marilyn had passed on just half a year prior and that there had been a service for her at Tassajara. It was sad news to hear and I wished I'd thought of contacting her much earlier.

I brought up with Leslie the possibility of getting Marilyn's material scanned and preserved better, something that I'd thought about for years. I was relieved to learn that Marilyn's friend Mark Stromberg had just recently contacted Keith to discuss making Marilyn's scrapbook more widely available. Before long I was corresponding with Mark and then Marilyn's son Larry Burns. Each of them sent me a PDF of slightly different versions of her book. Larry and his sister, Lee Doyle, wrote a touching remembrance of Marilyn that now resides on a page on cuke.com for her and this book (www.cuke.com/tass-marilyn). In it they wrote:

> She was, in many respects, while quite outgoing, a very private person. She was a maverick in all things, refusing normalcy, distrustful of the status quo. She loved gardens, but more so the notion of a hidden courtyard with thick overgrown ivy on high walls separating, as well as protecting her from the world at large. She was an intensely loyal, family-centric person who raised five children, two of her own and three from her second marriage.

> From the mid-1970s through the early 1980s, she traveled to Tassajara on weekends during the guest season—May to September. While practicing Zen, she began writing the history of the Hot Springs. She took to traveling widely in Monterey County at every chance, interviewing anyone and everyone who'd been part of the place, from the stagecoach drivers to the cooks. She documented conversations and stories, collected boxes of pictures, and passionately began writing an important part of California history with the skill of a scholar.

Now I find myself back again with Marilyn in the intriguing narrative of this book. I imagine times when there were grizzly bears, trappers, a creek full of fish, a narrow trail leading in just wide enough for a horse, the labor intensive building of the road, the early guests camping out in tents, the twelve hour trip in on the horse drawn stage from Salinas, the early cars, the bootleg whiskey guests would sneak in, the outdoor dance platform, the great old sandstone hotel, and the most evocative—contemplating the unknown thousands of years the Esselen and other Native Americans came for the sacred waters and purifying steam in sweat lodges.

Foreword

Marilyn had a clear eye and tells this story as it was told to her by people and news clippings—without any romanticizing or unnecessary elaboration. She did a good job on the final brief Zen Center section. I was at Tassajara from a few months after it was purchased and can vouch for most of what she wrote. I also checked things out with others including Tassajara's first head monk and Suzuki's virtual co-founder of the place, Richard Baker, the director for the first few years Peter Schneider, the first head cook Edward Brown who had worked in the kitchen there the year before Zen Center acquired it, Alan Yehudah Winter who was there very early on, and Leslie James for the later years. I found that people were delighted to be reminded of those early Zen days at Tassajara.

A meal chant used by practitioners at Tassajara has this line: "Seventy-two labors brought us this rice. We should know how it comes to us." Many labors likewise brought us Tassajara in unspoiled condition after being tended for millennia by Native Americans and for a century by immigrant stock. In Buddhism, caring for the physical space one inhabits is an integral part of the practice. Shunryu Suzuki said, "Cleaning is first. Zazen (meditation) is second." This book reminds us that while we may have brought a new spiritual lineage into that valley, it met there the ancient spirit of the place and the people who came before.

David Chadwick
March 18, 2018

Two main springs, Tassajara Creek, c. 1905

INTRODUCTION

IN THE EARLY 1970s I was working at a restaurant in Gonzales, California. The local farmers talked about Tassajara Hot Springs and all the wonders that had happened to them there over the years. I was strongly encouraged to go there. In 1971, four women friends and I headed for Tassajara in my 1958 Volvo. We made it almost to China Camp when the brakes went out and I had a flat tire. This was before cell phones, and the walk down the hill to the nearest help would be a long one, so we sat under a tree and waited for rescue. Along came a man in a station wagon who had been collecting pine cones up the road. After changing the tire, he put his car in front of mine and acted as my brakes going back down the hill. By the time we got to flat ground, the brakes were back and we were all exhausted and ready to go home. Tassajara would have to wait until later.

My first successful trip to Tassajara was in 1972. Everywhere I looked were wonderful old stone buildings. Being inquisitive, I wanted to know who had built them and why. None of the Zen students I asked had answers that were complete enough for me.

I went again in 1974 and met Jack Novcich at lunch. He was from Yugoslavia, spoke with a wonderful accent, and had quite a twinkle in his eye. He had lost his left arm and leg in a work accident in 1914 in Santa Cruz and came to the Springs almost yearly "for the waters." I borrowed a tape recorder and began my research with Jack that afternoon. His memories were priceless. He had owned Jack's Cigar Store since 1914, knew everyone, and the list of names he gave me of people to interview was long by the time I left him later in the day.

My early plan was to make a scrapbook for the desk at Tassajara. My husband was a schoolteacher in Greenfield, and he encouraged me to put it all together and see what came of it. As the years went by and I met with more and more people, I began to accumulate photographs, memorabilia, and reels and reels of taped interviews.

Life has its way of changing, and mine did. In 1983, I moved to New Mexico and began in a totally new direction. Tassajara history was put on hold.

Tassajara Hot Springs is about forty-five miles southeast of Monterey, California, in the Los Padres National Forest, at 1637 feet above sea level. It is centrally located in the Santa Lucia Mountain Range, between the Salinas Valley and the Pacific Ocean. At one location in Tassajara Canyon there are about twenty springs in the stream bed and along its southern bank. The temperatures range from 100°F to 140°F. An hydrologist working for the Department of the Interior stated:

> Hot springs will develop anywhere you have a heat source at shallow depths and faults in the crustal rock which allow water to circulate to depth and be returned to the land surface. The heat source could be either molten rock or proximity to the mantle due to a thin crustal plate.

In March of this year, 1998, I decided to end my segment of the Tassajara history in 1985. With that decision came the idea to make a copy of my manuscript and put it on the counter in the Tassajara office. A fulfilling end to a wonderful project, and here it is for your enjoyment and edification.

Hundreds of people shared memories, photographs, and information with me during the years I worked on this project. The time I spent with these people, and at the Springs, is a high point in my life. Often I recall an incident someone told me about Tassajara and realize how fortunate I've been to learn the history of the Springs. What a marvelous experience—to learn about Tassajara from the people who have loved it.

Santa Fe, New Mexico
May 8, 1998

Marilyn McDonald

NATIVE AMERICANS AT TASSAJARA

NATIVE NORTH AMERICANS were the first humans to enjoy the waters of Tassajara Hot Springs. The group called the Esselen made this area their home. Early ethnographers recorded an Esselen village at Agua Caliente, the Spanish name for hot spring, and although there is no evidence in the form of shell mounds or cooking fire remains that people actually lived at Tassajara, there have been people in the Santa Lucia Mountains for at least ten thousand years. These springs were certainly known to them.

Indians had many uses for hot springs: as a preparation for the hunt, as a place for renewing spiritual energy, and as a part of the male ritual of using a sweat lodge for deeply cleansing their bodies and ridding themselves of vermin. At Tassajara, a hut of branches covered with mud would be built over the spring in the stream bed, the site of the present-day steam room. The person would stay inside until he could no longer stand the heat, and then he would jump into the creek. Scraping the body with the rib bone of an animal to open the pores and clean the skin completely was the finishing touch.

About five miles upstream from Tassajara, at Church Creek, there are numerous caves that have been inhabited for at least thirty-five hundred years. Indians usually built their houses away from creeks to avoid flooding in the winter and to get away from gnats and mosquitos in the summer. When caves were available, they were much preferred as housing. It is also twenty degrees warmer on the side hills in the winter than on the valley floor.

Indian cave at Church Creek Ranch

I heard from the old-timers that the Indians used Tassajara to get well. Don't know if they lived there year-round, just that they got well. Took the baths and all.
—Oliver Williamson

In his *Handbook of the Indians of California*, A.L. Kroeber wrote:

> Long reckoned as an independent stock, the Esselen were one of the least populous groups in California, exceedingly restricted in territory, the first to become entirely extinct, and in consequence are now as good as unknown, so far as specific information goes—a name rather than a people of whom anything can be said. There are preserved a few hundred words and phrases of their speech; some confused designations of places, and a few voyagers' comments, so generic in tone as to allow no inferences as to the distinctiveness of the group.

[The Esselen, however, are not extinct. See Appendix, p. 149.]

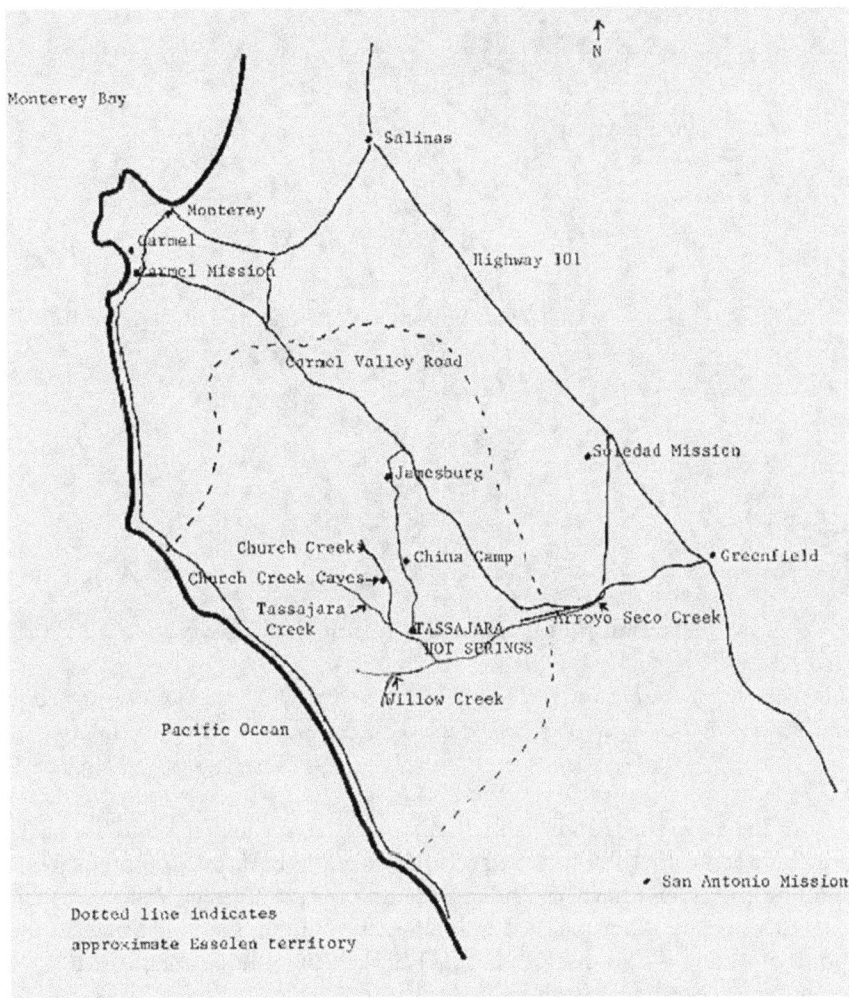

The founding of the Carmel mission in the 1770s brought the Esselen, a group ranging from one thousand to fifteen hundred individuals, into contact with white civilization—contact that resulted in their rapid decrease. By the early 1800s the missions at Carmel and Soledad had absorbed what remained of this small group.

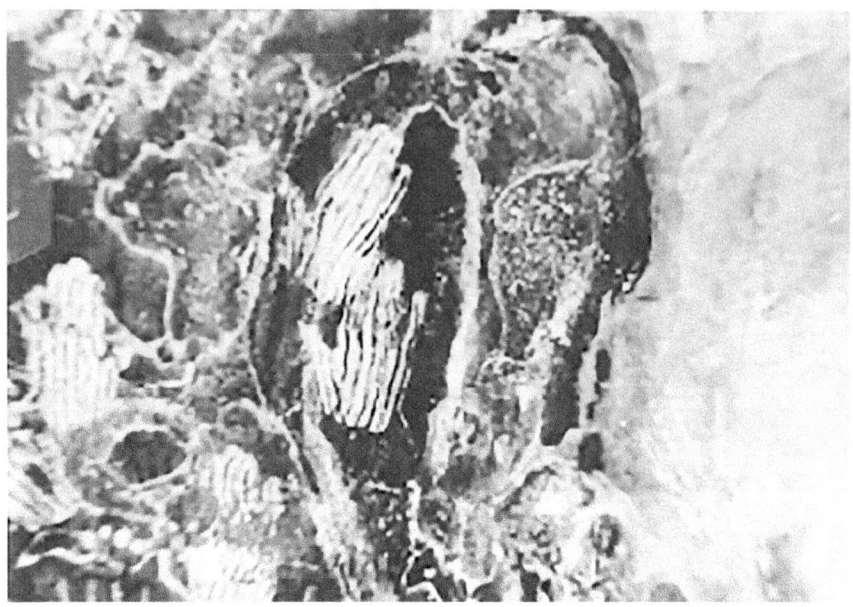

Indian pictographs at Church Creek caves

Many years ago sick Indians used to come all the way from Oregon to imbibe and bathe in the waters at Tassajara. They thought it was the headquarters of the Big Medicine.
—*Salinas City Index*, March 1877

In the early 1800s Indians from many different tribes came to Tassajara for the waters. In 1843 Jack Swan, while heading back to Monterey after a hunting trip, met a party of Indians coming up the Carmel Valley on their way to Tassajara. They planned to build a sweat hut at the hot springs in the hope of curing a skin disease that had broken out among them. In further describing the springs, Swan wrote at that time:

Frequently there would be several tribes there at one time, but because of the great abundance of wild game of all kinds, and fish, they had no trouble living.
—*Salinas Californian*, June 22, 1963

TASSAJARA HOT SPRINGS RESORT

THE NAME TASSAJARA is most likely a corruption of the Spanish word *tasajera*, which means a place where meat is dried, thus where jerky is made. Summers are often hot at the Springs, which makes it an ideal place to dry meat outdoors. In his book *California '46 to '88*, J.W. Harlan states:

> This tassajera was a log house with no windows — only a low door, and the meat was hung on strips of rawhide stretched across over a fire which smoldered on the middle of the floor.

The name Tassajara has been used through the years for more than one place in the area. There was a Tassajara School in Cachagua, the creek that runs through Jamesburg was called Tassajara Creek, and a place near Chew's Ridge was also known as Tassajara.

The Indians and the early travelers in the Tassajara area had the company of numerous beasts: foxes, bobcats, raccoons, coyotes, mountain lions, skunks, rattlesnakes, and an abundance of grizzly bears. The bears presented quite a problem because they often stood seven feet tall and weighed 850 pounds, and a single-shot rifle was usually inadequate for killing such a large animal. In 1861 in his book *Up and Down California*, William Brewer wrote:

> While speaking of animals — the grizzly bear is much more dreaded than I had any idea of. A wounded grizzly is much more to be feared than even a lion; a tiger is not more ferocious. They will kill and eat sheep, oxen, and horses, are as swift as a horse, of immense strength, quick though clumsy, and very tenacious of life. A man stands a slight chance if he wounds a bear, but not mortally, and a shot must be well directed to kill. The universal advice by everybody is to let them alone if we see them, unless we are well prepared for battle and have experienced hunters along.

Since settlers and grizzlies could not share the same area, hunters began to arrive at Tassajara. Rocky Beasley and his partner Joe Logwood camped at the Church Creek caves in the 1870s. They hunted grizzlies and sold the hides. Rocky boasted that he had killed one hundred and thirty-two bears.

Close to Tassajara are Bear Canyon, The Bear Trap, Bear Mountain, and Bear Trap Canyon. The Bear Trap got its name from a pit that was dug in the ground so the bear would fall inside. Bear traps made of white oak slabs bound with iron and built on runners were used to snare the bears and then take them to Monterey for bull and bear fights.

In the mid-1800s the repeating rifle was invented, and by 1900 grizzly bears were completely gone from the Santa Lucia Mountains.

> Rocky the hunter has again been heard from. On Monday before last, he and a man by the name of Logwood had an encounter with a huge grizzly bear in the San Antonio mountains, about thirty-five miles southwest of this city. It took five shots to kill the huge monster. After the first charge, he made for Rocky with his mouth wide open, but Rocky stood firm and gave him another charge. Still he advanced, and was within five feet of the brave hunter when he received his fatal and last charge. The ball hit him in the mouth and sent him in agonies to the earth. In another minute he would have had Rocky in his powerful claws, and would no doubt have crushed him to death. Rocky is not afraid of the devil, and often saves himself by his firmness and steady nerve alone. His name is becoming renowned.   —"Encounter with a Bear," *Salinas Weekly Index*, April 1, 1875

Tassajara's inaccessibility probably prevented regular trips by the early Spanish settlers in the Monterey area. In an 1869 report to the state surveyor general, the Monterey County Assessor made these comments:

> The healing qualities of a hot mineral spring which, although known since early days of the settlement of California, has been until now unappreciated ... there exists a large cave covered on the inside with Indian hieroglyphics ... near this cave and in close proximity to a fine mountain stream abounding in trout, is a sulphurous spring, the temperature of which is near 160°. This spring has lately been resorted to by persons afflicted with rheumatic complaints, and the effects, according to the testimony of those who have visited the locality, have been wonderful.

The Gold Rush in 1849, the completion of the Central Pacific Railroad in 1869, and the Depression of 1873 all brought people to the West Coast. With this increase in population, surveying the land became a necessity. Early land surveys in California and Oregon were often fraudulent. In Monterey County miles and miles of survey lines that were supposed to have been run were never actually surveyed at all. Faking survey maps was fairly easy. A map was drawn; trees, streams, and boundaries were added; and a bill for the work was made up and sent to Washington for payment.

A corner marker was set at Tassajara by John D. Hall, a surveyor who was eventually caught making fraudulent surveys and spent ten years in prison. A Salinas surveyor recalled:

> He set a corner here and there. He set one at Tassajara. He set one up near the top. In other places he said he set them, but there were whole townships where he only set one or two around in the places he could get to easily. They are supposed to set each section corner and each quarter corner round on the outside. Some of his maps show the streams running north or south and if you put the United States Government Survey Map on top you would see he wasn't even there. He didn't even know which way the streams were running. He just made up the corners. He never set any.—Leon Boling

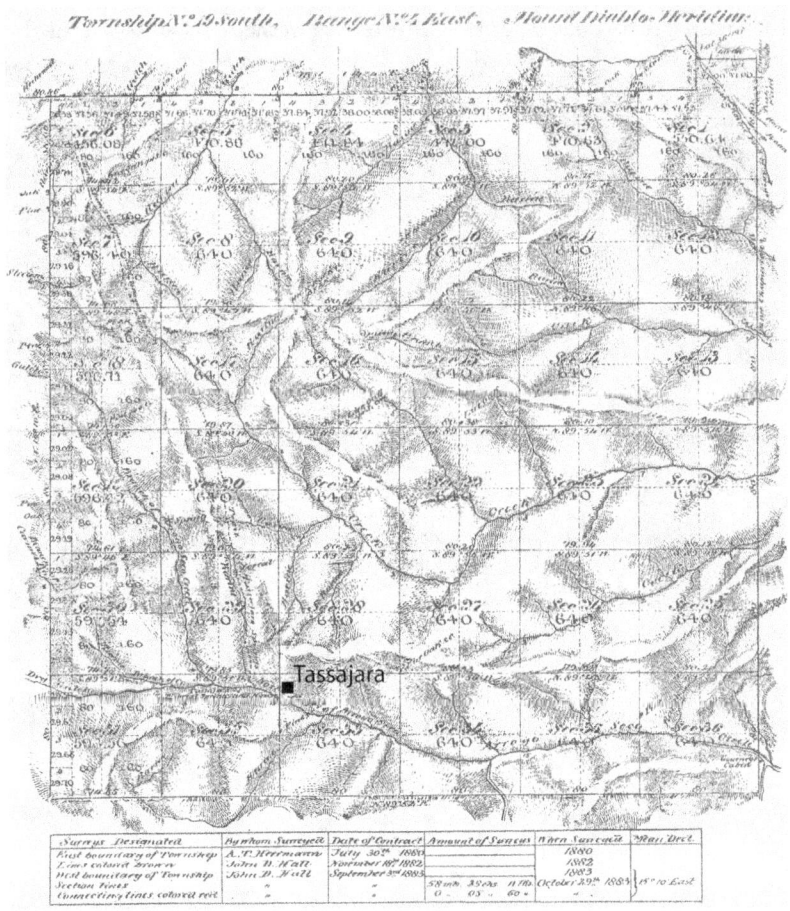

Fraudulent survey by John D. Hall

The early pioneers in the Monterey area found that much of the arable land was already taken up by Mexican land grants. Before dams were built, the land flooded in the winter and would be dry by April. The wind blew, the soil was hard, and wild mustard grew everywhere. Many of the settlers moved to the surrounding hills where there were year-round streams, no wind or fog, plenty of game, and abundant forage for their cattle.

Officially, J.E. Rust was the first settler at Tassajara. Records of a meeting of the Monterey County Board of Supervisors in June 1870 show that "the road to Tesajara Springs, being the same road laid out and traveled by J.E. Rust, et al." was declared a public highway on that date. This road was a trail scarcely wide enough for a horse to travel on. Why it was declared a highway is not known. Rust stayed at the Springs only long enough to build a small cabin, and then he moved on.

In 1875 J.B. Borden advertised in the *Handbook to Monterey and Vicinity*, describing "some dozen springs as effective remedial agents for all the ills that flesh is heir to." Borden had ideas about forming a joint stock company and improving the springs by building a hotel and bathhouses. He is credited with building the first shale rock structure.

L. B. AUSTIN,
ALVARADO STREET, MONTEREY, Next to the Express Office,
CIGARS, TOBACCO, ETC.
Candies, Nuts, Etc., Stationery, Blank Books, Show-Case Goods, Vegetables and Fruits.

TASSAJARA SPRINGS now Open to VISITORS

The undersigned gives notice that the Tassajara Springs are now open for Visitors. These Springs were noted centuries ago among the old aborigines for the Medicinal Virtues of the waters, and the pale faces are now adding their praises to that of the red man to the Great Spirit for the gift. Parties visiting the Springs can be furnished with meals, or, if camping, with provisions. Also, parties wishing to be taken to or from the Springs can be accommodated. Apply to   **J. B. BORDEN.**

W. H. PYBURN,
Keeps a First-Class Stock of
Groceries and Provisions, Wines, Liquors, Tobaccos,
Fruits, Candies, Glass and Crockery Ware.
The W. U. Telegraph Office. Hides, Game and Farm Produce Shipped.
ALVARADO STREET.

From *Handbook to Monterey and Vicinity,* 1875

In November 1876 Borden sold his squatters rights to William Hart, a sixty-one-year-old widower from Salinas. By March 1877 Hart had erected some buildings, put up some tents, and widened the trail in anticipation of the summer season. A young woman wrote this letter to the *Salinas City Index* in June 1879:

> In regard to the trail from James Ranch to the Springs, our party pronounce it in excellent condition. The country is very rough, but on a sure-footed animal one can trot at a brisk pace much of the way. We ladies think the horseback ride about sixteen miles, although Mr. Hart argues that it is only twelve. Much of the distance is through beautiful scenery—shady groves of oak and sycamore, interspersed with some fine specimens of madrone trees and a large variety of undergrowth, including the aromatic mountain laurel or bay tree, yerba santa, so valuable for its medicinal properties. There are several resting places on the route where travelers can quench their thirst at cold sweet springs, and let their animals feast on the luxuriant growth of wild oats found on the mountain sides.

Despite the remoteness of the Springs, many people still made the trip. On a June day in 1879 there were more than thirty visitors camping at Tassajara. Hart's cook, Mrs. Elliot, was known for her delicious food, which was brought by wagon as far as the James Ranch, where the perishables were put in the dairy house. Everything was then packed by horseback to Tassajara.

I am one of a party of campers who have pitched their tents within twenty yards of the finest medicinal hot springs in the State. The Tassajara Creek ripples along by our tent making very soothing music to lull one to sleep.... People are going and coming and many are repeating their annual trips, thus showing their faith in the efficacy of these waters.
—*Salinas City Index*, June 1879

Camping at Tassajara, c. 1900

Having spent three weeks at Tassajara Springs, owned by W. Hart, Esq., of Salinas, I desire to publicly testify to the wonderful curative properties of these Springs. I have visited most of the noted resorts for health in the Eastern and Northern States, but failed to realize any benefit. I came to California as a last resort and went to Tassajara Springs. I there found a climate as nearly perfect as it is possible to find on this continent, free from the chilling winds and fogs of the valley, and very exhilarating. After taking the second bath I found myself entirely free from neuralgia for the first time since last October and instead of any weakness from the hot bath, I gained steadily in strength and flesh. To those in search of health, I take great pleasure in recommending these Springs as possessing magical medicinal properties. Visitors may always be sure of courteous treatment from the proprietor. For amusement the streams abound with fine trout, and the mountains in wild game.

—A.T. Blaine, "Tassajara Springs: A Visitor's Testimonial,"
Salinas City Index, May 29, 1878

In July 1882 William Hart contracted to sell the Springs to J.W. Leigh. The price was to be three thousand dollars. Part of the sale was to be one of William Hart's mules. For some reason this sale never happened.

Hiking on the Tony Trail, c. 1900

Hart stayed at the Springs until October 1884, when he applied to homestead one hundred and sixty acres. During his nine years as owner he built several cabins and some rock buildings, planted a garden each year, and made a number of other improvements.

To be known abroad is all that the Tassajara Springs need to make them one of the most favorite resorts on the Pacific Coast. For general debility, asthma, cutaneous diseases, rheumatism and kindred complaints, their waters are said to work miraculous cures.

—*Salinas City Index*, March, 1877

Charles Quilty, c. 1890

Charles Quilty, who had been to Tassajara as a guest, purchased the Springs from William Hart in March 1885. The price was thirty-five hundred dollars, which included Hart's kitchen and household furniture, bed and bedding, and one hundred and fifty goats, more or less. Quilty planned to use Tassajara as a summer home for his family and friends.

Charles Quilty had married Mary Elizabeth Hagan in 1878. Her father, James Hagan, left her a great deal of money when he died. One of Quilty's grandsons, Charles William Jeffery, remembered:

Grampa Quilty was going to build that wealth all up and one thing and another. He had grandiose ideas, but everything he did fell through and he lost pretty near everything except the Springs. I don't know how, but he managed to hang on to Tassajara.

A native of South Carolina, Quilty had come west at an early age and received his education and practiced law in San Jose. He was president of the San Jose Light and Power Company and president of the Salinas Water Company, was associated with the Tulare Water Company, and for two terms was president of Pacific Coast Gas Association.

The Quiltys—Charles, Mary, and their seven daughters Gertrude, Irene, Mary, Pauline, Alice, Estelle, and Ruth—lived in San Jose. In the summer, they would come by train to Salinas, take a wagon to the James Ranch, and ride horseback to the Springs, where they stayed in one of the original log cabins.

Early log cabin at Tassajara, c. 1912
Club House beyond cabin

Postcard of people at the Narrows—undated

Charles Quilty, interested in investments with his wife's money, realized Tassajara's potential as a health spa. He took a partner, J.R. McPhail, hired Anthony Dourond as surveyor and superintendent of construction, and started work on a road from the James Ranch.

From the James Ranch to the summit at Chew's Ridge the road was mostly completed by horse-drawn plow; local laborers did the work. From the summit down, the work was done by hand with pick, shovel, and blasting powder. Charles Quilty hired Chinese laborers to complete this section. There were numerous unemployed Chinese miners and railroad builders in San Jose and San Francisco who would work for fifty cents a day and provide their own food. China Camp, on the Tassajara Road, is named after the workers who lived there during construction of the road.

In many places the roadway had to be blasted out of solid rock and for long distances the lower side of the grade is supported by a perpendicular wall of loose stones constructed for that purpose.   —*Salinas Weekly Index,* October 1888

Tassajara Road, c. 1900

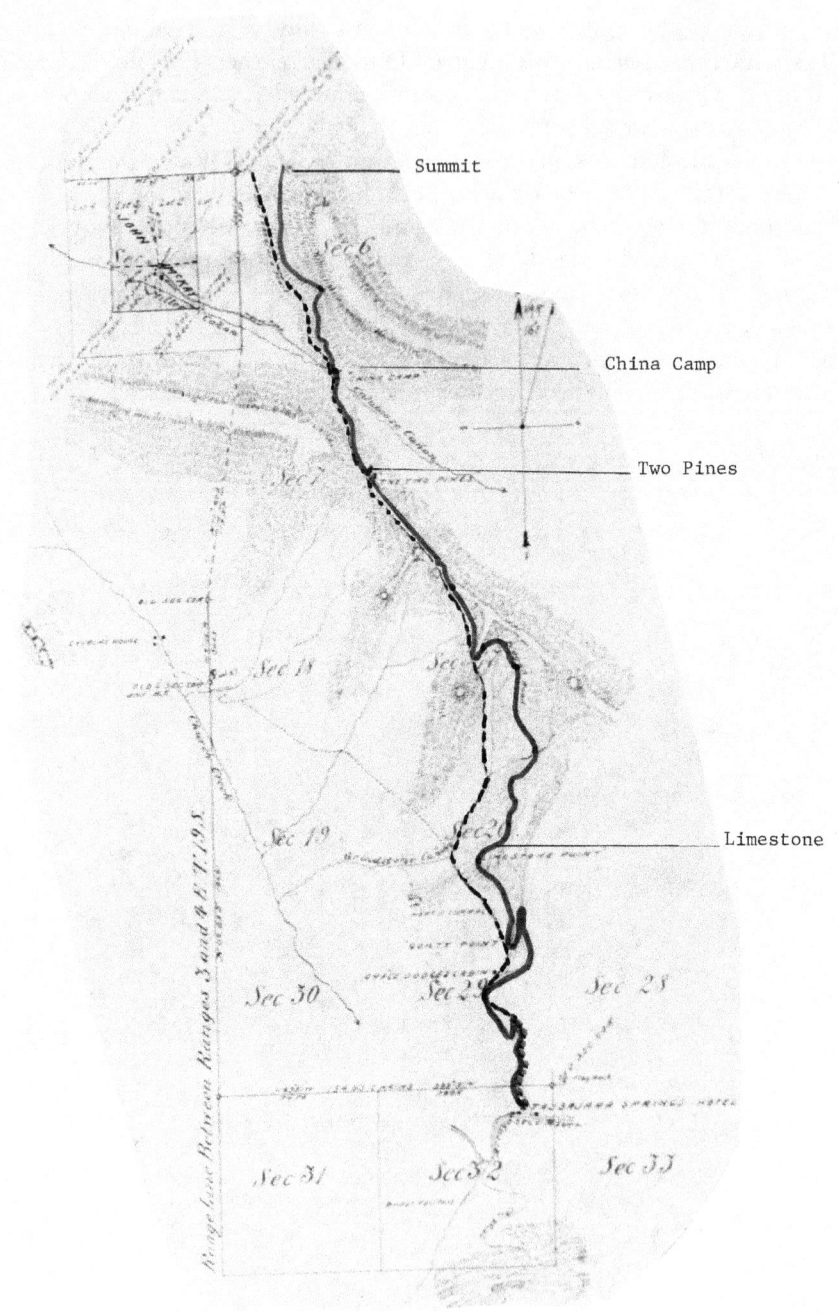

Map of road from Chew's Ridge to Tassajara
Dashed line–Indian trail
Solid line–road

Tassajara Road, c. 1914

If a hunk of stone was too big, you would blast it in two. If you couldn't handle it then, you'd blast it again. Then probably get a pry bar and roll it off to the edge by prying it over. It was all hard work, no doubt about that. But, they were used to hard work in those days.   —Robert Arnold

The road was officially opened in September 1888. It cost Quilty over eleven thousand dollars to build. W.J. Hill, editor of the *Salinas Weekly Index* and mayor of Salinas, was the first passenger who went all the way to Tassajara in a wagon. He said, "Just before reaching the Springs we were signaled to a halt, when half a dozen blasts were fired as a salute of welcome and to proclaim the completion of the road." There were thirteen guests plus a stonecutter, a woodcutter, and a cook present on the eventful day.

Because there was no regular stage, a Mr. Lewis, who carried the mail from Salinas to Jamesburg, would take passengers on to Tassajara for four dollars each way. He left Salinas at eight a.m. on Saturday and stayed overnight at his ranch near Jamesburg, arriving at the Springs on Sunday around noon. By 1892 a regular stage service was in operation. The stage left two boarding houses in Salinas, the Abbott House and the Jeffery House, every Tuesday and Friday morning at 6 a.m. The route followed the Monterey Highway out of Salinas, then went over the Laureles Grade and down to Carmel Valley. The four horses were changed at Whitlocks, changed again at the James Ranch, where the passengers had lunch, and then the next stop was Tassajara. "The horses knew the road," said Ira Bailey, an early passenger. "They went down practically by themselves."

The finished road was fourteen miles long and just barely wide enough for a wagon to drive on. "If you think it's straight down now, you should have seen it then," Irma Reaves remembered. There were parts so steep that the men would get out and walk to save the horses. Only the ladies would stay in the stage and ride. Side curtains were installed to keep the ladies from seeing how far it really was to the bottom. The saying was, if you were well enough to stand the ride in there, you didn't need to go.

The Tassajara Stage, c. 1900

I'll never forget it as long as I live. I was scared green. Mr. Hallock was the stage driver. He'd come up to one of those hairpin bends and set the brake and swing the horses. Then let out the brake and off we'd go. I said to my momma, "I'm scared," and she said, "Well, get under the blankets and say your prayers." —Irma Reaves

Tassajara Hot Springs Resort

Tassajara Stage, c. 1900

They had a log at the top that they shoved through the back wheels when they started down—called "putting a fetlock on it." It'd drag and not be a strain on the horses. Then they'd haul the log back up to the top and be ready for the next trip down. They also had a big pile of old shoes at China Camp they'd nail on the pedal brake to help hold the wagon back. —Ira Bailey

Salinas Weekly Index, June 1890

At the bottom it reads:

> Stage leaves Railroad at 8 a.m. every Saturday, stays over night at Jamesburg and arrives at the Springs Sunday noon.
>
> Returning—Leaves Springs Thursday, stays over night at Jamesburg and arrives in Salinas Friday afternoon.

[For larger negative see Appendix, p. 150.]

Maintenance of the new road was a monumental job. Winters are often severe in the Santa Lucia Mountains, and each spring Charles Quilty found that the road needed to be practically rebuilt. In 1891 he petitioned the Monterey County Board of Supervisors to declare Tassajara Road a public highway. For some reason, the fact that the road had already been declared a public highway in 1870 was ignored, and in June 1891 his request was granted. Since that time, maintenance has been handled by the county.

J.T. Pollock's horse and wagon on Tassajara Road early 1890s
[Pollock's ad & photo close-ups are in Appendix pp. 151-153.]

Charles Quilty hired an Italian cook and charged a dollar per day to eat in the dining room. He charged three dollars per week for camping privileges and three dollars per week for use of the baths. The Church family, who lived upstream at the caves, supplied milk, butter, eggs, cheese, and some of the meat. Tassajara was advertised as having the best food that could be obtained, with plenty of fish and game.

Early dining room (left) and stone bath house (right), c. 1890

The *Salinas Weekly Index* reported in October 1888:

They have a little garden along the creek near the bathhouses. It is about thirty by a hundred feet, and produces large quantities of melons, corn, onions, carrots, red peppers, tomatoes, etc. Hot water is used for irrigation, and melons of the second crop have been ripe for a month past.

In 1888, with the road completed, the Quiltys turned their attention to building a hotel. Sandstone was chosen as the building material because of its abundance in Tassajara Canyon. The property had many large boulders that were blasted and cut on the site. There may also have been some sandstone brought from a side canyon up the road. Charles Quilty hired Henry Arnold of Jamesburg to blast the rock and cut the blocks, and most likely he hired Italian stonemasons from San Jose to help with the cutting and Chinese laborers to help with the actual building. Given the location, it was quite an impressive structure.

If they had a big rock they'd drill a hole and put a charge of powder in it. I can remember my dad with an ax with a blade about three inches wide. He just chipped the edges off those blocks. —Robert Arnold

Tassajara Hotel, c. 1892, Henry "Harry" Arnold, builder

> I remember seeing him handle those big blocks. He built it up kind of in stairs. Rolled the block over one and then over the next 'til he got it to the top, where he wanted to place the thing permanently. Then he'd go down and get another block. You had to watch yourself handling them — if one got away, they were very heavy.
> —Robert Arnold

A kiln was constructed to burn lime rock, quarried up the road, for use as mortar in the building of the hotel. Emil Rossi, a Salinas stonemason, explained how mortar was made in the early days:

> Bake the chunks of limestone on a railroad tie fire for a couple of days. Dig a hole and put the cooked stones in the hole and add water until the limestone is the consistency of lard. Renew the water for a few days keeping the lard-like consistency. Then age it for about thirty days until it is the consistency of cottage cheese. The more age, the stronger it gets.

The finished mortar was mixed with sand and water, and sometimes a bit of horsehair or straw was added before putting it between the stones.

The completed hotel had forty rooms and was built in an L-shape. Rooms were small and furnished with a double bed, dresser, washstand with pitcher and bowl, and a thundermug (chamber pot). There were eight outhouses in back of the hotel near the little creek. All interior wood—window frames, floors, and doors—was redwood. The floors were covered with Japanese mats. There were two parlors, one for men and one for women, each with a fireplace. There was no heat in the individual rooms.

When there were more guests than could be accommodated in the hotel, a tent was pitched behind the building.

Back of hotel with a tent set up for extra guests, c. 1900

Jeffery House, c. 1900

Carr Abbott, c. 1917
by Tom O'Hara

Quilty leased the Springs to Carr Abbott of Salinas, who opened the new hotel for the summer season of 1893. The rates were ten or twelve dollars per week for boarders, and three dollars per week for campers. The horse stage left the Jeffery House, at the corner of Main and Alisal Streets in Salinas, on Monday, Wednesday, and Friday, returning Tuesday, Thursday, and Saturday. The trip took twelve to thirteen hours and cost four dollars each way.

Across from the hotel, almost straight up the hill, was a box in the ground with a lid. Inside was an old iron bed spring. Old-timers with a mischievous sense of humor would send the new people up to get a pitcher of water from the "iron spring."

He'd look for a likely one as they got off the stage. "I can't get up there, but maybe you can for me." They'd get up there and find a bed spring.

—Ira Bailey

The Iron Spring, c. 1915

At a drinking water spring, c. 1890

They called the water granite wine. When seasoned with pepper and salt and a little butter, it tastes like chicken soup. —*Salinas Weekly Index*, October 1888

Two main springs provided hot water for bathing. In early times, water was brought across the creek to the bathhouse in a wooden flume. In 1906, when the new plunges were constructed, water was piped to the holding reservoir, then into the plunges. The same system is in use today.

Postcard with the two main springs, c. 1890

Magnesium Spring, c. 1895

In 1895, when I was about six, there was a spring across the creek. People use'ta drink it. I'm sittin' there, and of course everybody don't know it, but I had a hole in one shoe. I pulled my dress around it so it wouldn't show. —Mae Cahoon

Magnesium Spring, c. 1915

The Magnesium Spring is one of the drinking springs. Although a 1977 analysis showed barely a trace of magnesium, it was treasured through the years for its magnesium content. This spring is situated downstream from the men's plunge.

Stone bath house, c. 1890

A two-room bathhouse was constructed in the 1870s. One room had a wooden bathtub suggestive of a horse trough. The other had a hole in the ground that was cemented up and called the plunge. Water was brought across the creek in a wooden flume and the temperature regulated to suit the individual bather. In the late 1800s Quilty added more rooms and installed porcelain tubs.

October 1888, *Salinas Weekly Index* bath directions

The modus operandi is as follows: Leave the water as hot as you can stand it—say from 90° to 115°. Stay in it from fifteen minutes to half an hour. Drinking as much of the hot water as you can swallow in the meantime, which ought not to be less than two quarts. You will then be pretty well heated up. Now come out of the water and roll yourself up in a couple pairs of woolen blankets and sweat for half an hour or so. The perspiration will emerge through the pores of the skin and roll off in great drops, making the blankets almost as wet as though they had been dipped in water. Rub dry and dress yourself, after which some light exercise, say a few minutes walk should be taken before setting down for any length of time. Repeat every day and drink plenty of the hot water. You will soon feel the beneficial effects. If the sweating process should weaken you too much, do not take it every day, but do not fail to drink plenty of water.

Reservoir at the back of stone bath house, c. 1890

Stone bath house, c. 1900

Kitchen and dining room, c. 1890

A combined kitchen and dining room, built in the 1870s, may have been the oldest building at Tassajara. This building burned down in April 1978. The kitchen was on the left, the dining room on the right, with swinging doors between. It was built of shale rock taken from the mountain opposite the plunges, with hand-hewn alder rafters and a roof of split shakes. When Quilty built the hotel, this building was remodeled and made larger to increase dining capacity. A new kitchen was added in back, with a complete basement for storage.

The original structure of the Club House building from the 1870s was probably the basement and first floor. There were three doors on the north end of the first floor that may have been entrance doors when the building was first constructed. Quilty was probably responsible for building the retaining wall and most likely used soil from the hotel construction area as fill, creating the flat area between this building and the present-day kitchen. The second floor was built around 1900 and used for staff housing. In 1905 Quilty obtained a liquor license and turned the first floor into a bar and card room called The Club.

The Club House, c. 1910

South side of the Club House—dining room 1982

Pipe runs hot spring water to the swimming pool to take the edge off the cold spring water. It's removed for the winter before the creek rises.

Hotel veranda, c. 1905

Undated postcard

The steam room, or vapors, as it was called, was a redwood shack that was built in the stream bed where a hot spring rises. The rocks in the stream bed were moved to create a pool, and a canvas tent was erected. A person could come out of the steam room and jump into the creek in the privacy of the tent. In the spring, as soon as the winter runoff in the creek had subsided, they would put the shack and tent in place. The shack had room for four people, and the recommended steam time was ten minutes, with twenty minutes being the absolute limit.

Young kids would go up the side hill and peek in the hole in the tent where the steam went out—they could see the naked ladies sittin' on the bench. —Anonymous

The ladies hung their sun bonnets outside as a signal that it was occupied. One man hung a bonnet outside as a joke and none of the men got to use the steam room all day. —Laura McGregor

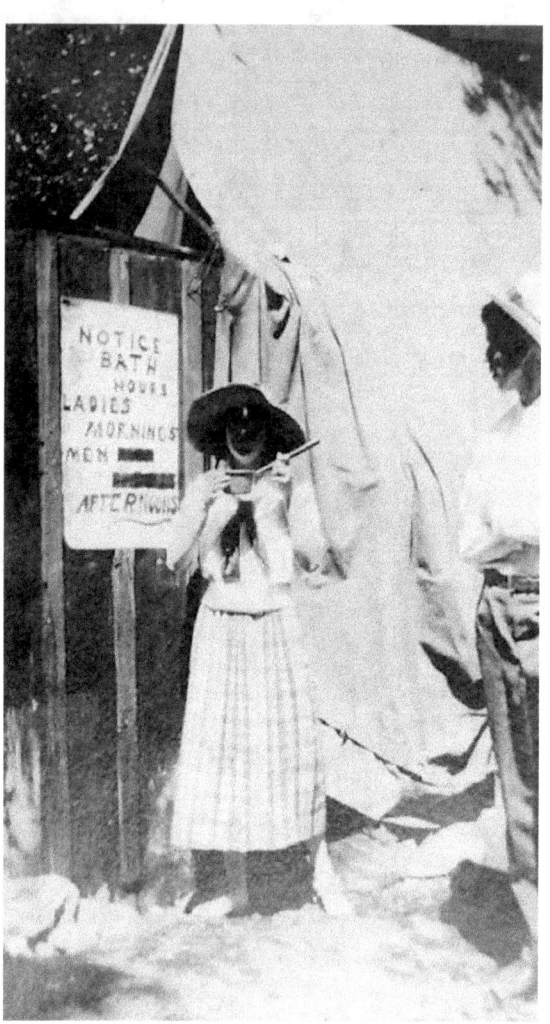

The steam room and tent, c. 1910

Plunges and steam room with tent, c. 1906

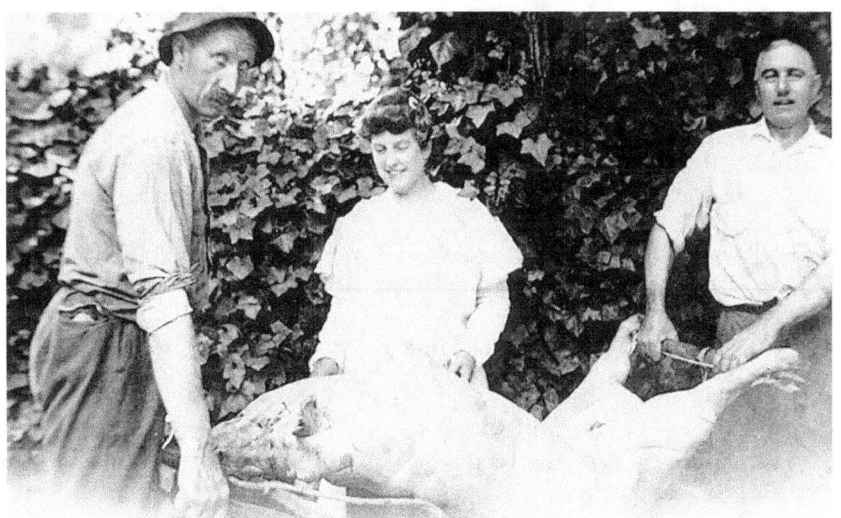
Helen Quilty, helpers and pig, c. 1906

They said if you dropped an egg in that water under the steam room, it would be boiled in two minutes.
—Ira Bailey

The water was so hot that I've seen them scald chickens, turkeys, and pigs in it after the season. The sweat house set right over that. And it was a sweat house! Built of wood so it could be taken down every winter, otherwise the creek would have washed it away.
—Paul Clinefelter

PACIFIC GROVE REVIEW: 12/12/93 (1893)

A POINTER ON TASSAJARA
MRS. EDITRESS OF THE REVIEW

A brief sketch of a recent trip to Tassajara Mineral Hot Spring may not be uninteresting, particularly if you contemplate a visit to that wonderful locality. On Dec. 5th a tenderfoot and a half tenderfoot procured from the stable of Mr. Kent that noble bay horse Sam and a buggy and started for, to them, that terra incognita, Tassajara Springs.

Passing through Monterey, with its modern buildings interspersed with old adobes, we ascended the mountain which divides Monterey from Carmel bay. At the summit we stop a moment to take a view of Monterey Bay to the north and beautiful Carmel Bay to the south. Here we leave the 17-mile-drive and take the county road down to the Carmel Valley. Leaving Pt. Lobos Road near the old San Carlos mission, we follow up the pretty Carmel river valley, passing many dairy and fruit ranches, until we reach Stephan's ranch house and hotel combined — 18 miles from Pacific Grove where the stage from Salinas to Tassajara changes horses and the passengers dine. The proprietor is a ready talker and so is tenderfoot. Immediately they get into an argument. Our host discusses the beautiful climate, mountain scenery and rich valleys. Tenderfoot claims that the price of the climate, with land thrown in, is exorbitant — out of all reason. The discussion is kept up evening and morning and when the last word is said the question remains undecided.

Leaving our jolly host in the morning the way leads up the river to a point three miles below the dam of the Pacific Improvement Company, from which the pure, clear, cool water is piped to Pacific Grove and Monterey. The better road leads up the Tularcitos via Jamesburgh. We were directed to take the plainest traveled road. Unfortunately for us a drove of cattle had passed up and obliterated the wagon tracks, leaving the plainest road over a mountain by way of Cachagua. The distance was about the same, but more mountainous, causing us more foot travel to favor our good horse. We started out for sightseeing, and we had considerable of it, but we cannot linger in describing the scene, lest we take too much of your time and space.

We arrived at 1 p.m. at Messrs James and Chew's, another stopping place where the stage changes horses, sixteen miles from Stephan's. Here we found agreeable company with old time Californians and miners in the early '50s. We did a little in that line ourselves long, long ago, and had old times brought to recollection. After a pleasant rest we started early in the morning to climb mountains and cross canyons. Our way lay three and one half miles up a mountain, then along a divide with deep canyons on either side. Then up we go over San Lucia peak, 5,000 feet above the ocean, the highest point reached. Pretty soon we approach the range overlooking canyons converging at the springs. Here the view is indescribable — a heterogeneous conglomerate of rocky mountains and deep canyons. What an awful stress of nature when this upheaval occurred. Mirabile visu! Mirabile dictu! John Muir and Clarence King, eminent as they are, would find a picture worthy of their pen. For six miles we descend along the side of mountains and around heads of canyons until we arrive at

Tassajara Springs. Here a sad mishap befell us. The season was over and the hotel left in charge of a man devoid of the milk of human kindness. Not a bite of horse feed would he let us have at any price. His plea was that he needed it all for his own horse. Here we were at 1:40 p.m. sixteen miles away from that terrible region over which we had walked half way to save faithful Sam. Tenderfoot was anxious to start on our return, fearing we would have to camp out overnight, giving Half-Tenderfoot scarcely time to visit the bath house and springs to test their instantaneous curative properties, for it was impossible to remain in that present inhospitable region.

How is it here are nearly ice cold and hot springs so near together? There must be fires down below; friction won't heat water.

At 1:50 p.m. we start on our return, walking most of the way, leading the horse up that steep six-mile grade. There is only one house between the Springs and James' where we hoped we might stop overnight. But we reached it, we found it locked and the proprietor gone. It was now dark, and three and one half miles down the mountain. It is not a pleasant experience to walk and lead a horse with a buggy down such a mountain by starlight and feel for the road, especially where the evergreen trees overlap the branches and shut out the light. Nevertheless, we arrive safely at the hospitable house from which we started in the morning, with somewhat tired legs and sore feet. Faithful Sam, for who we entertained mercy and pity, relieved our feelings by exhibiting less weariness than ourselves.

From the James Ranch to Pacific Grove is a fairly good road by way of Jamesburgh, with no long or steep mountains to climb. The moral to be learned from this trip to Tassajara Springs is that unless one proposes to walk a considerable part of the way, don't take a single horse and buggy, but a pair, two pair, or go by the stage from Salinas.

Tassajara Road, c. 1898

Tassajara Hot Springs

Hot Magnesia Springs, Temperature 120 Deg.

Hot Sulphur Springs, Temperature 150 Deg.

These wonderful hot medicinal springs are now open for the season. A new two-story sandstone hotel furnishes accommodations for guests. Stone plunge baths and porcelain tub baths, with unlimited quantities of hot mineral water for bathing and drinking.

Infallible Cure for Rheumatism, Liver and Kidney Troubles,

Skin Diseases and Like Complaints

Altitude 1600 feet. Grand scenery, fine fishing and hunting.

Rates: $10 and $12 per week. Campers, $5 per week. Good barn accommodations.

Arnold & Bruce's Stages leave Salinas at 6 A. M. every Monday, Wednesday and Friday, arriving at Springs at 6 P. M., returning the next day. Fare, $4 each way. For particulars address

H. ARNOLD,

Tassajara Hot Springs, Monterey Co. Or C. W. QUILTY. San Jose, Cal. m8-2m

---

Daily Evening Owl, **May 1896**

Place was quiet. A nice place to go for a rest. And brother, after that ride you needed a rest. —Irma Reaves

In 1891 Mary Quilty legally claimed the water from a point about a mile up the road. Pipes were laid and water for drinking was brought to the Springs.

The Quiltys established a post office at Tassajara in 1892. The post office proved to be a poor idea because even if there were no passengers, the mail had to be brought all the way to Tassajara anyway. In 1894 the post office was moved from Tassajara to Jamesburg.

From 1894 to 1896 Henry Arnold leased the Springs from the Quiltys. Arnold had learned the stonemason trade while serving in the German army and did a major part of the stone work on the hotel. In 1887 he married Sarah Church. During the building of the hotel Sarah got pregnant. Quilty offered to remember the child in his will if they would name it Tassajara. Born in May 1894, he was the first non-Indian child born at the Springs and was named Henry Wallace Arnold.

During the winter months Arnold cut wood, built stone terraces and walls, and did some preliminary work on an alternate road downstream. Charles Quilty's idea was that people would come in on the Tassajara Road and go out downstream through Arroyo Seco to Soledad. This route would have been much easier on the horses and the passengers.

Tassajara Road Petition, October 1894

To the Honorable Board of Supervisors of Monterey County, California:-

    Your petitioner respectfully asks that your Hon. Board appoint Henry Arnold, lessee of Tassajara Hot Springs, to care for the Tassajara Road from Jamesburg to the Springs, a distance of about 16 miles, during the winter months until March, 1895, which he will do for the sum of Thirty ($30) Dollars.

    The work to be done, being the cross ditching of the road every 200 feet, so as to prevent the washing away of the road, also the removal of rocks and land slides, opening cross streams and gullies, and looking after bridges.

    He will go over the road from time to time during winter, and keep it in good condition, so as to save expensive repairs in the Spring.

    Mr. Arnold has leased the Springs for the next season, he lives right on the road, and can look after the road better than a person from a distance, who will lose time in coming and going to the scene of work.

    Furthermore, Mr. Arnold is derectly interested in keeping the road in as good repair as possible, so as to be ready early for the next season business.

    All the receipts of the Springs, and more too, are left yearly in Monterey Co., and the visitors coming and going to the Springs make business for hotels, saloons, groceries, livery, and other business in Salinas, and Monterey County.

    In view of the above, I trust this petition will receive your favorable consideration.

Dated Oct 22 1894

Respectfully yours,

From the records of the Monterey County Board of Supervisors

In April 1897, shortly after the birth of the Quiltys' eighth daughter, Genevieve, Mary Quilty died of heart disease. She was thirty-eight years old.

The Oksens, James and Emma, were hired by Charles Quilty in 1898 as caretakers. James was also the butcher, cabinetmaker, and masseur. Emma was the masseuse. In 1905, their first child, Irma, was conceived at Tassajara. They nicknamed her "Tassy."

The Oksen family lived year-round at the Springs until the end of the season in 1908. For many years after that, they travelled from Watsonville to Tassajara in a camp wagon that James Oksen built. After a three-day trip getting there, they would spend three or four weeks camping.

The Oksens' campwagon heading for Tassajara, c. 1915

In 1898 Charles Quilty met Helen Ford, a San Jose schoolteacher. Born in San Francisco in 1872 and orphaned at a very early age, she was raised by her grandparents, the Ryans of Gilroy, California. When they met, Quilty was forty and Helen was twenty-six. Helen's family was opposed to the marriage because of the age difference and the fact that Quilty already had eight daughters. Despite the wishes of her family, their marriage took place in Gilroy on April 21, 1899.

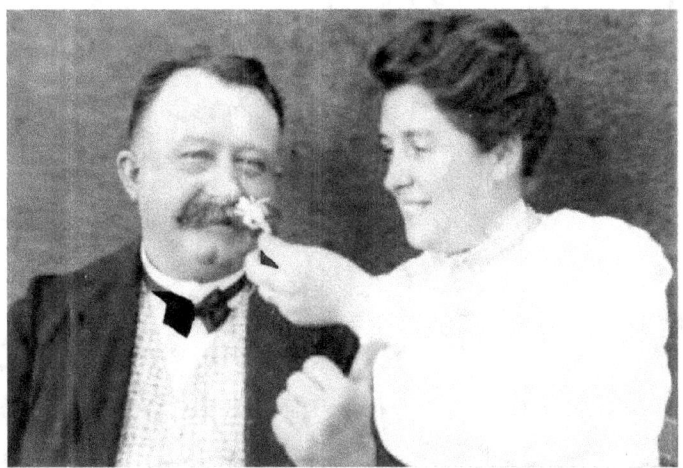

Charles and Helen Quilty, April 21, 1899

Bill Jeffery, from Salinas, leased the Springs and the Tassajara Stage Line from the Quiltys in 1900. He paid two years in advance on his lease, which was six hundred dollars the first year and seven hundred dollars the second year.

Jeffery attempted to increase business at Tassajara by advertising, building a bowling alley with two maple lanes, remodeling the baths and the dining room, and making improvements around the grounds. He installed refrigeration for keeping food fresh, but also so he could supply ice for drinks—a big success with the guests.

Jeffery was concerned that someone at the Springs would become ill while he was in charge, and the nearest doctor was fifty miles away. He took precautions, bought a book called *What Everyone Should Know*, asked questions of the doctors and dentists in Salinas, and tried to prepare himself for accidents. One evening a Miss Sanborn of Watsonville seemed to be having a heart attack. Jeffery was afraid to give the heart stimulant he had on hand for emergencies, so he saddled a horse and rode the fifty miles to Salinas in ten hours to get help. While changing horses at Jamesburg his latigo strap broke and he fell into a rose briar bush. He went back to Tassajara on the stage the next day, found Miss Sanborn feeling much better, without any treatment, and was immediately faced with a new emergency: Joe Daga had accidentally shot himself in the groin and Jeffery had to turn right around and take him to Salinas in a wagon for treatment.

One of the Quiltys' eight daughters, Mary, found Bill Jeffery very attractive. The Quiltys wanted her to wait, but in August 1901, Mary Quilty married Bill Jeffery. The combination of the road, the hotel, and Bill and Mary Jeffery was a winning one. At Tassajara, they began a long career as very successful hotelkeepers.

Bill Jeffery, c. 1900

Bill and Mary Jeffery, c. 1901

TASSAJARA HOT SPRINGS

WILLIAM JEFFERY, Proprietor

This famous health resort is now open to the public. The camp grounds have been repaired and enlarged. There is a large dancing platform, and other appurtenances for the benefit of guests. The road over the mountain to the springs has been put in good shape for travel.

The table will be supplied with the best the market affords, including fish and game.

BOARD AND LODGING

Including baths, $10 and $12 per week. Camping privilege, $2.50 per week.

The place will be kept in first-class style, and no pains will be spared by the proprietor for the comfort and pleasure of guests.

REGULAR STAGES RUN FROM SALINAS

From Official Souvenir Booklet of the 34th Encampment, G.A.R., Pacific Grove, 1901

G.A.R.—Grand Army of the Republic—organization of Civil War Union veterans

That weather up there had a lot of effect on a lot of people. Moon shinin' every night, hammocks all over the place. A number of marriages in Salinas and Watsonville were the result of meetings at the Springs. —Harry Koue

Guests, c. 1910

Guests, c. 1914

Salinas was such a small town in those days, everyone knew everyone. Tassajara was one of the places to go and we all went. —Ella Enevoldsen

JOHN MORROW'S LETTER.

Describes His Trip From Santa Cruz to Tassajara.

Ed. "Sentinel":—At 6:30 A. M. on the 20th we left Santa Cruz for this place. We ate lunch and rested for an hour a few miles south of Watsonville. The entire distance traveled this day was one continual hay crop and fruit orchard, with once in awhile a thrifty field of beets. Hay balers were busy everywhere, and after entering the Salinas valley I found steam threshers at work on both sides of the road.

On the morning of the 21st, at 8 A. M., we bid good-bye to our accommodating hostess, Mrs. Jeffery Granger. We crossed the Salinas river on the big iron bridge, and followed up the Toro creek about 5 miles over a level, but slightly sandy road. The scattering timber here is mostly sycamore and buckeye and some large oaks. The land is mostly used for dairying purposes. After going up and over a hill for about two miles, we came to the point where the road to Tassajara leaves the main road to Monterey, which is ten miles distant and nearly due south.

We took the Tassajara road, winding around the mountain side, always up grade, until we reach the summit between Toro valley and the Carmel river. From this road we had a fine view of the Salinas valley and Toro creek valley clear up to Mount Gelaspu. In this valley we could see a number of ranches and a neat white schoolhouse nestling among the large, spreading oaks. One of the ranches with a fine orchard is the property of Mr. Leibbrandt, formerly of Santa Cruz. On reaching the summit we had a fine view of the famous and almost sacred Carmel valley. The old padres had a happy way of giving Bible names to all beautiful places, and how appropriate it was that they should give this historically beautiful, if not hallowed, name to this lovely river and valley, for who has not heard of Mount Carmel as mentioned in holy writ?

After descending the mountain on a good grade we came to the Carmel river on the rancho called Los Lauralis. Then we follow the river and valley for many miles until we reach Jamesburg. This burg consists of a house and barn, with a postoffice attachment. All along this road are stock ranches, with plenty of cattle and horses. Some hay is raised here, but not much else. About a half a mile beyond Jamesburg we camped for the night under an oak tree and near the creek and a large barn. This is called the Lewis ranch, and we were much surprised that this Mr. Lewis is the father of Charles Lewis of Santa Cruz, and we were still more surprised to see Mr. and Mrs. Crowe of Santa Cruz standing on a little knoll above us looking down at us and watching us arranging our camp among the trees. Well, we were very glad to meet them in this lonely, romantic, out of the way place. They came down to our camp and we spent a pleasant evening talking about Santa Cruz and other things. We had traveled this day 28 miles over a most beautiful and interesting country, which is well worth the trip to see. The next morning we were up at 5 o'clock feeding the horse and cooking breakfast and getting ready for a start, for we had now a seven-mile mountain to go up and quite a steep grade, too, but this was only a beginning to 15 miles of about as wild and rough a piece of grand old mountain scenery as I have ever had the pleasure to see. Last summer I was in the heart of the Sierras, but now I am in the heart of the Monterey mountains and I find much here that is grand, beautiful and wonderful, as well as in the Sierras.

We left camp at 6:30 and began to climb the seven-mile grade to the summit of the mountain, which divides the headwaters of the Carmel river from the headwaters of the Arroyo Seco river, which runs east and empties into the Salinas river near Soledad.

I will leave ourselves climbing this mountain, the summit of which is 4,900 feet above sea level, and after we have gained the summit and rested I may write some more and try to describe still more of the wonders and grandeur of these majestic old mountains. JOHN MORROW

Tassajara, July 25th.

John Morrow's Letter:
Santa Cruz Evening Sentinel, July 28, 1901

The following letter from same paper August 9, 1901
[See Appendix p. 154 for another letter.
See www.cuke.com/tass-marilyn for easier reading.]

JOHN MORROW'S LETTER.

Describes His Trip to Tassajara Springs, Where His Tent is Pitched.

Ed. "Sentinel":—My last letter ended as we commenced to climb the mountain, which is seven miles to the summit, the grade about 16 inches to the rod or what would be called a 11 per cent grade. We were just three hours going up this seven miles. The mountain is quite well timbered with mostly black oak and some underbrush. From 6:30 to 9:30 A. M. much of the road is shaded by the trees. It is a hard, but very interesting trip. There was much holding of the brake to keep the surrey from going backwards. While the horse rested sometimes I would walk behind and block the wheel. The road is very narrow, with very few places where another team could be passed, but on the last thirty miles of our trip we never met any one on the road, either afoot or a horseback, or in any other way. We had the road, the rugged mountain peaks, the deep canyons and rocky gorges and all this grand panorama of majestic scenery all to ourselves, with no one to dispute our rights. All nature was quiet, grand and beautiful.

From the summit we had a view of the road for the distance of about two miles. It follows a dividing ridge between the Carmel and Arroyo Seco rivers. This ridge has scarcely any timber, but is covered with what I call black brush or chaparral. The altitude, 4,960 feet, being rather high for much timber. I noticed here many of what is commonly called the Spanish dagger in full bloom. In the summer time they send up a stalk from 8 to 12 or 15 feet high, and the trunk or stalk is from 2 to 5 or 6 inches in diameter, and when in full bloom with their white flowers they may be seen here and there on the steep mountain sides at least a half a mile away. And what is most strange, they do all this without a drop of rain and apparently without moisture of any kind. This being the extreme head of two rivers running in opposite directions, of course the country is much broken up by gulches and canyons running in every direction, and this makes many sharp ridges and rocky peaks, which add much to the beauty and grandeur of the scene before us.

At the southeast end of this ridge we can look away down into a deep canyon where runs the north fork of the Arroyo Seco, which is quite a large stream. Here on its banks are located the Tassajara Springs and hotel. One would almost believe that he was looking down into a gorge below the level of the sea. And now to get down to the hotel and springs we have to make a descent of 3,260 feet over a wonderfully picturesque piece of road. It winds in and out and around many sharp rocky points. It is built on an even grade the entire distance, but narrow and quite steep. There is considerable timber, mostly black oak, which furnishes plenty of shade on a hot day.

We put on the brake and down we go to the bottom of the deep canyon always in view. By degrees we get lower and lower and nearer to our journey's end. My right foot gets tired holding the brake, then I change and use the left. And when I reach the bottom of the grade at Tassajara Springs, the tires on the hind wheels are so hot that I dare not touch them.

It was an interesting ride and rather exciting. A four-horse stage goes over this road and clear through to Salinas every day, hauling passengers to the springs safely and without accident, but any one who rides over this route, either by stage or their own conveyance, will not soon forget it, for it is an exciting, interesting, grand and beautiful ride. About halfway down this grade we halted for an hour or more at a clear, cool spring by the side of the road for dinner. Here we boiled potatoes, fried bacon and eggs, made coffee and ate with good appetites, and Dolly horse also had a good appetite for hay and rolled barley. After this needed rest we started on with only three miles to go, all down grade. So we were soon at Tassajara Springs, the stone hotel and camp ground and the end of our journey for the present.

I always try to avoid arriving in a new camping place with all hands hungry, because mankind is like animals in this respect. When they are hungry they are liable to be cross or out of humor. We arrived at 2 P. M. and soon selected a camping place, set up our tent under some trees and were at home once more. This place is 53 miles from Salinas by wagon road and 30 miles on an air line. It is nine miles to the coast on an air line, ten miles to Paraiso Springs and eighteen miles to Soledad, all on an air line. It has been estimated that a good wagon road could be made from here to Soledad, following the Arroyo Seco down by Mr. Abbott's place and the distance would be only thirty miles. Some people here tell me that it is only five or six miles following the creek to Mr. Abbott's place, and he has a road from his place to Soledad. Wouldn't this be a grand fishing trip to fish from here down through the canyon to Mr. Abbott's place? But it must be some one younger than I am to climb, tumble and scramble over all those rocks and driftwood. This is a good creek to fish in. It is very swift and rocky, and is larger and carries more water than the Soquel creek. But I am tired now and perhaps will write more some other time.

JOHN MORROW.

Tassajara, July 28th.

John Morrow, c. 1900
(author of letters on previous pages)

Helen Quilty, c. 1904

Charles Quilty's second wife Helen decided she wanted to run Tassajara. In October 1903 she discovered that Bill Jeffery had not officially recorded the lease he signed with Charles Quilty. The Quiltys went to Tassajara to evict Bill Jeffery. Helen told him that they wanted him to leave. He said, "OK, if that's how you want it." That night after everyone had gone to bed, he jumped on his horse and rode to Salinas, and the first thing the next day he had his lease recorded. He made his point, but since he was married to a Quilty daughter, and life with his in-laws would have been unpleasant, he gave up his lease, and he and Mary moved to Salinas.

In 1904, Helen and Charles Quilty took over the management of Tassajara. Charles Quilty decided to pursue his idea of continuing the road downstream. The petition that he presented to the Board of Supervisors in 1904 stated:

> The opening of the proposed new road would make the Springs accessible to a large class of invalids all over the coast who cannot stand the present trip. It would also give access to a country which is very attractive to campers and sportsmen by reason of its splendid hunting, fishing, and scenery.
>
> —Records of the Monterey County Board of Supervisors

In July 1904, Lou G. Hare, Monterey county surveyor, headed a survey team between Tassaraja Hot Springs and the Piney Creek Post Office, downstream about twelve miles from Tassajara. This survey showed that a major portion of the road would have to be blasted out of solid rock. The cost would have been enormous, so the road downstream was forgotten for the moment. Field notes by Lou G. Hare of the Tassajara-Piney Creek Survey of 1904 are available at the Monterey County Road Department in Salinas.

[Some of Hare's field notes are in the Appendix pp. 155-158.]

Lou G. Hare, c. 1904

Traditionally, mineral waters have been used for their curative properties. Egyptians, Greeks, and Romans had their municipal baths, and throughout history mineral water has been used for aches and pains and relaxing of muscles. At Tassajara, people took the baths and the steam, drank lots of water, ate good food, rested and enjoyed the country air, and went home rejuvenated and ready for the next year. People from the surrounding area—Salinas and Watsonville, Castroville and Monterey—came to Tassajara. They brought their families and their friends.

TASSAJARA HOT SPRINGS

TO meet the public demand for information concerning the marvelous Tassajara Mineral Springs, this folder is issued. A handsome illustrated pamphlet descriptive of the Springs is now being prepared. The Springs are in the heart of the Santa Lucia Forest Reserve, Monterey County, near the head waters of the Carmel River. The road up the Carmel River from Monterey to the Springs is a beautiful and picturesque drive. At present the stage for the Springs leaves Salinas every Monday, Wednesday and Friday morning, landing passengers at the Springs in the afternoon of the same day.

The Springs are eighteen in number, and vary from cold to 145° in temperature.

The late Dr. Canfield, of Monterey, was a great enthusiast over the Springs, and being for years a regular correspondent of the Smithsonian Institute of Washington, forwarded waters from the different springs for analysis. The Institute reported that the Tassajara were the most remarkable Mineral Waters ever submitted for analysis, and equal to any mineral springs then known.

The quantity of water is practically unlimited, and sufficient to supply the wants of thousands. The Springs burst from the mountain sides, and pour their thermal waters into the Arroyo Seco Creek. A beautiful waterfall of three hundred feet furnishes nonmineral pure mountain water for domestic use. The Arroyo Seco is a large mountain stream abounding with fish. A large lime quarry is on the ground. The owner of the Springs burns lime for building, while an inexhaustible sandstone quarry furnishes the stone. The hotel, houses, hot water tanks and plunge baths are all built of stone.

The waters are a positive cure for stomach, kidney, liver and rheumatic troubles, and a specific for all cutaneous diseases. Nervous trouble of all kinds is cured by the mild influence of these waters.

The most remarkable feature of the Springs is the Radio Vapor Thermal Bath over a boiling mineral spring, which affords a luxurious and exhilarating bath.

A two-story sandstone Hotel furnishes first-class accommodations. Hunting in the neighboring mountains is good, and four large streams furnish unexcelled trout fishing.

The climate is unsurpassed, the Springs being only eight miles from the Pacific Ocean, with high mountains between, which shut off the fog. The altitude is 1650 feet above the ocean level. Those who have visited the famous springs and watering places of Europe and the United States, declare that the Tassajara Hot Springs, in their combination of marvelous mineral waters, glorious California climate, altitude, and mountain streams, surpass them all.

The limited space of this folder will not permit the publishing of the cures effected by these waters. It is sufficient to say that all who have visited the Tassajara Hot Springs have been more than satisfied. The charges at the Springs are $12.00 to $14.00 per week for boarders, and $2.50 each per week for campers, which includes use of baths, waters, grounds, etc. Campers can purchase supplies at the Springs. Each visitor should bring his own sweat blanket.

The stage fare to the Springs is $4.00. Stage leaves Salinas Monday, Wednesday and Friday mornings. Everything is conducted in a neat, plain manner—no style. If you are sick in body, here you will find a cure; if worn and weary in mind, here a solace and rest. ⌀ ⌀ ⌀ ⌀ ⌀ For pamphlets or further information, address,

TASSAJARA HOT SPRINGS, MONTEREY COUNTY, CAL.

Brochure, c. 1905
gift from Robert Beck

In 1906 a new bathhouse was built on the south side of the creek. It was divided into two parts, one for men and the other for women. Each side had two private tub rooms and a large plunge. A reservoir was constructed in order to cool the hot springs water before it was piped into the plunges. Massage rooms were built upstairs.

Bathhouse, c. 1906

Large metal tank in center, below bath house

The walk from the hotel to the baths was called Kimono lane. All the ladies had kimonos, some from Japan, some homemade. Everyone tried to have the prettiest one.
—Ella Enevoldsen

Kimono Lane, c. 1915

Ladies at Bath House, c. 1906

When I was young and shy I went into the plunge. The women were going in without their clothes. It was terribly hot water. There were stairs going right into this deep water. Nothin' to hang on to that I can remember. You just walked an inch at a time down those stairs. I stayed in there and all of a sudden I started to get funny in my head. They dragged me out of there in a hurry. Out on that porch. Someone had some smelling salts. I don't think I ever went in those plunges again after that. —Ella Enevoldsen

Relaxing at Tassajara, c. 1925

In those times men of wealth and position often travelled alone. Marriages were arranged by parents and were oftentimes formal affairs. The wife would go to Santa Barbara with the children and the nurse. The husband would go to Tassajara to hunt, fish, and relax.
—Mrs. MacLean

The common man, c. 1915

Business people, especially doctors and lawyers, were so formal in those days and they just loved it there, sitting around in their shirtsleeves. —Mrs. Juhler

Sitting in their shirtsleeves, c. 1925

One time a billionaire named Foster stayed for five weeks. Just came as a common man.
—Richard Westphal

The Hotel, c. 1905

Dear Friend, It is just glorious here. I drink all the mineral water I can. There are four kinds. And three kinds of baths. I take hot vapor baths and cold plunges. They are so good. I am feeling much better. I have no aches here. It's so hot you don't feel like doing much. My boys are with my mother. The roads are dangerous here and I don't want them to come in. I have to dress for dinner so will close. Our meals are swell and I eat all before me. Best regards.

[written on the back of the postcard below]

Hot water springs, c. 1905

In April 1905 Charles Quilty sold the Tassajara Stage Line to his wife, Helen, for $10. This sale included two stages, twelve horses, twelve sets of harnesses, and all the accessories, together with the business of the stage line. She had the right to stable the horses on the grounds at the Springs without charge, although she had to furnish all feed and maintenance.

In August 1905 Charles Quilty sold Tassajara Hot Springs to Helen— sold for "love and affection," and no money changed hands. In July 1906 Helen sold it back to Charles, also for love and affection. Why these sales took place, for no money, is not known.

In March 1909 Charles Quilty again sold Tassajara Hot Springs to Helen. The price this time was eight thousand dollars, plus assumption of the mortgage. This price included the Springs, one hundred and sixty acres, and the Horse Pasture, also one hundred and sixty acres.

Around 1910 Charles Quilty had an accident while driving on the Tassajara Road. The combination of being overweight, a heavy drinker, and breaking his leg led to complications that caused his death four years later on September 20, 1914.

J.C. Anthony driving Tassajara Stage with Helen Quilty, c. 1905
[Used with permission from Mayo Hayes O'Donnell Library, Monterey]

After the death of her husband in 1914, Helen Quilty became totally involved in Tassajara. She had never-ending ideas for things to do. If someone came to the Springs and they weren't doing anything or didn't know anyone else, she stepped right in and put them to work shelling peas or snapping beans, as a group project. With her natural flair for business and genuine liking for people, she was just the person to be in charge. People rarely took advantage of her.

She was an exceptional shot. Use'ta sit on the hotel porch with a .22 and shoot across at the squirrels. She could outshoot most of the men. —Paul Clinefelter

She was an exceptional shot, a hell of a poker player, and a good judge of bourbon. Everyone liked her. —Bill Lambert

Helen Quilty and guest drinking water at the Magnesium Spring, c. 1905

By 1910 automobiles were becoming the popular way to travel. There were no paved roads, no service stations, and the driver had innumerable obstacles to face. Whenever he drove his car, he had to carry tire patch kits, tire chains, gasoline, oil, boards (in case the car got stuck in dirt or mud), ropes, etc. It was traumatic to drive anywhere, much less on Tassajara Road, which was considered the worst road in California.

Helen Quilty decided that even though Tassajara Road was difficult at best, a four- or five-hour automobile trip would be an improvement over the twelve-hour horse stage ride to the Springs. After leaving Tassajara in 1903, Bill Jeffery bought a livery business in Salinas. Helen Quilty hired him to drive people to Tassajara in his two 1913 Cadillacs.

A person who went to Tassajara in the early 1900s had to really want to go.
—Ira Bailey

Model L Touring Car at Tassajara, c. 1910

One of the first cars driven to Tassajara: a 1909 "30" shaft-drive Model L Touring Car with special headlamps. —Henry Clark

Bill Jeffery's Cadillac, c. 1914

They were havin' a convention at Hotel Del Monte. The chef planned crawfish. Ordered them from Oregon. They came in big tubs by boat. The boat was late. Didn't land 'til the day after the convention. What to do with all those crawfish? Tanks of 'em. Pop Ernst said, "Let's take 'em to Tassajara." They went in a 1909 automobile. Nobody went to the Springs in cars in those days. They brought the crawfish in and dumped them in Tassajara Creek. Those crawfish worked their way down to the Arroyo Seco. There's still lots of 'em. That's where they started, the first crawfish in all of Monterey County.

—Anonymous

Tassajara Hotel, c. 1912

In 1914 Helen Quilty started negotiations for a scheduled automobile stage with Ira Bailey, an employee of Bill Jeffery.

Ira thought seriously about the idea of running an automobile stage to Tassajara. He recalled, "Everyone said no car could stand the trip over that road on a regular basis. A man didn't have good sense that he would think about puttin' on a commercial run on that terrible road, but when you're young, nothin's impossible."

Helen Quilty and Ira Bailey worked out a contract that paid him eight dollars per month to carry the mail, six dollars per person one way or ten dollars per person round-trip stage fare, and fifteen dollars per 2,000 pounds for freight. Ira and his drivers also received board and room while they were at the Springs.

TASSAJARA STAGE LINE

LACEY'S GARAGE IRA C. BAILEY, PROPRIETOR

SALINAS, CALIF., _____ 192

Ticket for the Tassajara Stage

Bailey bought Bill Jeffery's Cadillacs, and on opening day in May 1916 he drove his first automobile stage to Tassajara. In the beginning he drove in every other day. By the second year business had increased and he added another stage and started making the trip in and out every day. He sometimes had his two Cadillacs and the extra car in service. John B. McKinney, a cabinetmaker in Salinas, built two nine-passenger stage bodies that fit on the frames of the Cadillacs.

Tassajara Stage, c. 1917

Those old Cadillacs—nothin' like 'em. Radiator was copper. All the lead pipes were copper or bronze. Copper is the best conductor of heat, you know, those things just get up boilin' hot. Stop a minute, let 'em tick over slowly and they'd cool right down. We didn't pay much attention to the outside of the stages, but we always kept the copper and brass shined in the engine. —Ira Bailey

Most people, whether they know it or not, have a bit of a fear of claustrophobia. That was my feelin' the first time I ever went in there. About 1910, on the old horse stage. Got down in there and just felt like—you look up all around you and you're just closed in like the bottom of a well. I couldn't get out of there fast enough. That's the way most people felt about it. The old road, before they made the improvements, was such a—they were scared to death after they got in there. Even when they went in on the auto stage. —Ira Bailey

> It was such a scary road that people got in there and although they wanted to go out you couldn't hire 'em to go 'til they got their courage back. By that time, the charm of the place got hold of 'em and they wanted to stay on. —Ira Bailey

Bailey took his job seriously. He wore special Italian driving gloves, and he and all his drivers wore uniforms. Part of his interview with a prospective driver was a ride to the Springs; there was no better test than the Tassajara Road. The top driver was paid two hundred fifty dollars per month, plus food and lodging at the Springs.

Ira Bailey, 1916 by Tom O'Hara

> There was one place goin' up Tony's Boulevard where the stage would stall real easy. I'd stall just to give the passengers a thrill. "Well folks, I can't start here," I'd say. "Guess I'll hav'ta back down the grade a ways." People would have been chattering and chattering and all of a sudden there'd be absolute silence. They'd be afraid to stay in and afraid to jump out. On the off side you could look way down there and no place to stand if you did jump out. The driver of the stage had no problem with people talkin' to 'em, especially after he left Jamesburg. —Ira Bailey

Occasionally a person would drive his own car into the Springs. By the time he arrived, he would be so shocked by the road that he would hire Bailey to drive his car back out for him. The charge was five dollars to drive the car up to the Cascades. Bailey remembered:

> If I'd charged 'em fifty dollars they'd have gladly paid it. That road, rock and shale, barely wide enough for one car to stay on it, too much for most people. One time a woman went over the edge at Lime Point. We found her car at the bottom, all crushed and mangled. We never did find her. Figured she was eaten up by mountain lions. I can't recall the name of the fella—use'ta stand by at the hotel with a team o' horses in the early days when the cars first started comin' down there—the Fords—he knew he'd hav'ta pull 'em out. Made his livin' that way.

Tassajara Auto Stage, c. 1917 at Tassajara Hotel

Telephone Stop, c. 1930
Sign reads: "Autos Stop, Telephone Tassajara Hot Springs," and road rules.

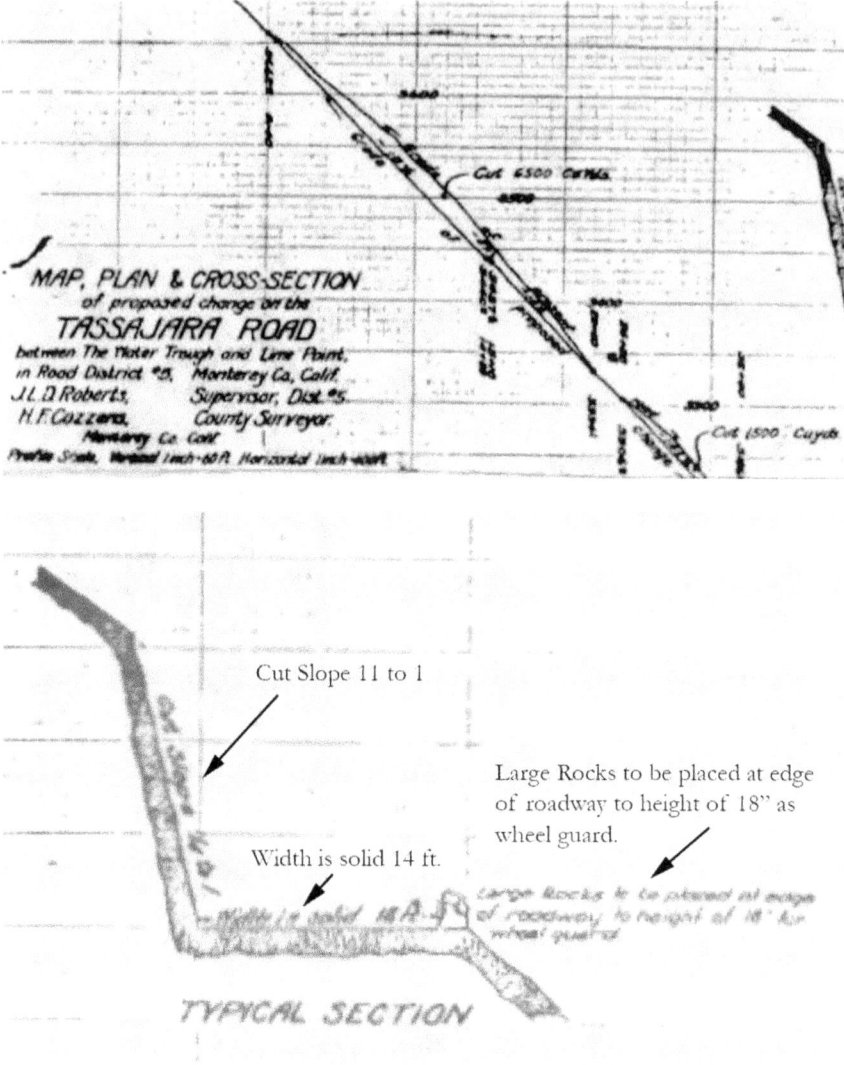

From Monterey County Road Records
[See more in Appendix p. 159.]

They was very careful drivin'. Anyplace there was danger—just crawl and put on the low gear. Keep the brakes in perfect condition. Every time when the stage leave Salinas the brakes is check. Tires was check. Everything 100 percent before begin. The road was one way. Use'ta be a telephone at the summit. Call up. If anybody comin' up—you stay right there. You no move 'til those people pass. When they pass, you start down. That was for years run that way.
—Jack Novcich

In the early 1920s the Monterey County Board of Supervisors decided to make some changes on the section of the road called Tony's Boulevard. They removed the steepest parts and widened the road. Ira Bailey recalled, "I enjoyed the daily challenge of seeing if those old cars would pull the load up Tony's Boulevard. Chains were required, winter and summer on the Boulevard because of the grade and the loose rock roadbed. We had special ones constructed with a cross chain in every link."

Bailey often had eight passengers, plus twelve hundred pounds of luggage and freight. In the early years of the stage, he also hauled all the food. Bailey knew how to pack everything in and still leave a little room for the passengers. The driver coming in to Salinas in the morning would leave orders with the butcher and grocer, who would deliver to the stage depot at the Jeffery Hotel. Helen Quilty was always very concerned that Bailey charge her accurately for freight. Everything was weighed as it was taken off the stage. On return trips Bailey would tuck gallon bottles of water from Magnesium Spring in around people's feet. He sold them in Salinas for a dollar each. Bailey recalled:

> Mrs. Quilty was an awful gossiper. I've always been close-mouthed. I never paid any attention to what went on in the stage or who was in it or anything else. She'd invite me to her office for a drink and try to pump me. Wanted to know all about everybody. I had enough to do takin' care of a load of passengers — lookin' out for their safety. I wasn't listenin' to any gossip. She resented that, but I had an iron-bound contract. I could always express my opinion, and I did.

Tassajara Road and stage, c. 1920

The discharge point for the stage passengers was in front of the hotel stairs. Everyone would gather at arrival time so they could see who was coming on the stage.

Waiting for the Stage c. 1917

"About 5 p.m. you'd hear him comin' up about three hundred yards away and someone'd holler, "Stage," and we'd all run out to see who was comin' on the stage."

—Paul Pioda

Above—from a page in Marilyn's scrapbook

Guests at hotel steps, c. 1915

They'd be all hot and dusty from the ride in and we'd be sittin' there all clean waitin' for them.   —Elita Hawley

The staff, c. 1910

We'd always say, "We'll meetcha' at Tassajara." Sometimes I'd stay two months. Oh, we had such a good time. I don't think there was anyplace anybody could have a better time than at Tassajara. You knew everybody. It wasn't a lot of strangers you were with.
—Mrs. Menasco

Guests at hotel, c. 1915

There were very few children up there. The ones that brought 'em always knew the limits right away. Mrs. Quilty saw to that. —Harry Koue

People went not just one year, but year after year they'd go back. A lot of them came because of the waters, you know, the curative powers. —Rose Rhyner

Guests at hotel, c. 1920

Heading for the baths, c. 1925

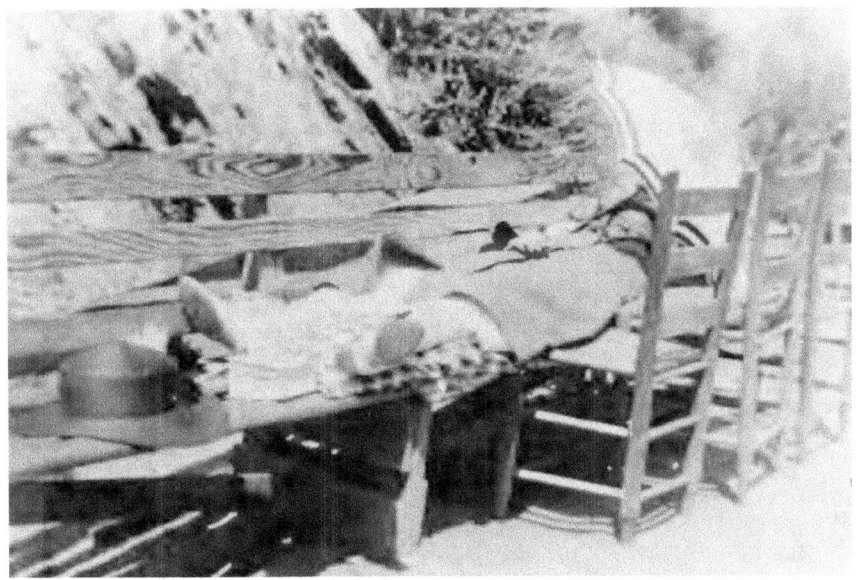

Mamie Whalen resting, c. 1917

Mamie Whalen, she was from Watsonville. Used to be up there for the whole season. She'd come up there and was so stoved up with rheumatism she had to walk with a cane and crutches. When she left she threw them away. That's how good that place is for health.

—Harry Koue

Everyone would be out on the veranda of the hotel after dinner sittin' around visiting and we'd go into different ones' rooms. If there was some kind of crabby old fussy butts, we'd fix up their room. We'd put a French sheet on the bed. A half sheet. They get in and they can't get their feet down. We did that. We put crumbs of crackers in the beds. There was an old maid fussy budget school teacher. Prissy little voice. She'd bring back these—"Oh, this is the most interesting specimen of flower"—weeds or somethin'. We weren't interested in wildflowers or weeds. We fixed her room up. We'd take a pillow and stuff it underneath the blanket so it'd look like a person was in bed. We called it "man in her bed." Us young folks—when the stage would go back—we'd all chip in some money and have them bring us a watermelon on the trip in. They'd put it on ice. Then at night we'd get it and go up to the Flats and make a bonfire and talk and sing and have this watermelon. Take a bath towel and tie it around our chin. Just good clean fun.—Ella Enevoldsen

A Poem by Ira Bailey and William Handley
c. 1920

Tassajara, land of sunshine, where the sparkling, healing rills,
Burst from out your rocky fastness, antidote for human ills

Where the mountain jay's harsh chatter ushers in the dawning day,
While among the swaying tree-tops, blithesome squirrels leap in play

Where the graceful water willow makes obeisance to the stream,
As beneath the dancing riffles, darting troutlets flash and gleam

Where the truant mountain breezes bear a fragrance sharp and sweet,
From the sage and manzanita, and the gnarled and grey mesquite

Where the rugged granite boulders strive forever with the foam,
Of the rushing, restless brooklets, hurrying to their ocean home

Where the cliffs in savage grandeur guard the smiling vales below,
Decked with verdure in springtime, pale with winter's wreaths of snow

Where the mescal flings to heaven, shafts of purest, dazzling white,
And the madrone's glistening leaflets, wink and dimple in the light

Where the shade and sunlight mingle by the mountain streamlet's brink,
And at eve the forest dwellers shyly venture forth to drink

Where the stars blaze out in brilliance as the firmament grows dim,
While the moon in silver splendor, stoops to kiss the canyon's rim

Backward winging thoughts possess me, as in retrospect I see,
Happy crowds that used to gather underneath the "gossip tree"

With the pleasant summer playtime slipping lazily away,
Til it all too soon had vanished like a wisp of driven spray

And I know, when next the poppies gild the slopes above the sea,
That again I'll hear the calling, Tassajara calling me

The automobile stage was a complete success. Business increased, and in 1917 Helen Quilty had a telephone and telegraph installed in the hotel. In 1919 she had nine cabins built across from the hotel. When they were completed, she had nineteen more built down the lane toward the barn. The bowling alley was converted to quarters for the help, and a laundry was constructed near the barn. There were accommodations for two hundred people.

On January 15, 1918, Helen Quilty bought the Pines property from G.P. Hansen for ten dollars. Tassajara Hot Springs now included the Pines, the Horse Pasture, and the Springs property, a total of four hundred and eighty acres.

From the records at the Salinas Courthouse, Salinas, California:

Tassajara Hot Springs 160 acres was homesteaded by William Hart in 1884. Charles Quilty bought this property in 1885. The Horse Pasture 160 acres was granted to Loly Tharp in 1855 by the U.S. Government as "bounty land to certain officers and soldiers who have been engaged in the military service of the U.S." Tharp was the widow of Joseph Tharp, Private in the Revolutionary War. She assigned the property to Wilburn McPhail in February 1892. In December 1893, McPhail sold it to Charles Cockrill for two hundred and fifty dollars. In June 1894, Charles Quilty bought the Horse Pasture from Cockrill for two hundred and fifty dollars. Quilty included the Horse Pasture when he sold the Springs property to his wife, Helen, in 1909. The Pines 160 acres was homesteaded in 1894 by Grace McPhail. In 1916 she sold it under her married name, Grace Dodge, to G.P. Hansen. Hansen sold it in 1918 to Helen Quilty.

Helen Quilty hired a Chinese cook named Sam, who had a callous on his thumb so thick that he used it to test oil to see if it was hot enough for cooking. Guests who were camping would come to the kitchen to purchase a loaf of bread from Sam, and whoever was the fortunate one would always be given a big chunk of pie along with the loaf of bread. One guest recalled:

He use'ta make the greatest pies. So us kids—in the evening one of our entertainments was to sneak in the back of the kitchen and steal a piece of pie. He was a jolly old fella—kinda' short and heavy. Scared the devil out of you if he caught you. —Paul Pioda

Sam was the cook for many years. No one knows where he came from, or where he went, but they certainly remember the wonderful meals he prepared.

Mrs. Quilty asked me, "How's Sam getting' along?" "You wanna' know the real facts about that?" I sez. "He's a very good cook and he makes good pies—but you know what he does—you get so much berries in there that they mold, so he puts a bunch of sugar in there and stirs them up along with the mold." I sez, "It don't make any difference in the flavor as far as that goes though." —Paul Clinefelter

Sam the Cook, c. 1917

Stage arrival area, c. 1915

Dining room, July 4th, 1912

Dinners were often elaborate affairs; at times as many as eight separate courses were served, with clean dishes for every course. A seat was assigned when you arrived. Helen Quilty, famous for her matchmaking abilities, always seated a young lady next to a young man she thought suitable. On special occasions the tables were moved to the center of the dining room or out under Gossip Oak. There were usually two or three entrées. Most of the meat was grown on the property. They had chickens, a milk cow, and sometimes hogs. There was always a big fish fry at the beginning of the season.

Talking of appetites leads me to remark how perfectly voracious guests become between the combination of mineral waters and good food. I was there three weeks, and I never will forget the A-1 meals that were served, not once, but right along. Even the guests on crutches were not far behind in the race to the dining room when the gong sounded. —*Salinas Weekly Index*, April 1911

Dining under Gossip Oak, c. 1910

In his book *Ragtime*, E.L. Doctorow wrote:

The consumption of food was a sacrament of success. A man who carried a great stomach before him was thought to be in his prime. There was a heavy traffic to the spas and sulphur springs, where the purgative was valued as an inducement to the appetite. America was a great farting country.

TASSAJARA IS HUMMING HAPPILY

EVERYBODY THERE GETS ALL THAT'S COMING

BELATED REPORT OF THE GLORIOUS FOURTH, FEAST AND FUN

Tassajara, July 16.—Fourth of July was one scream from daybreak until the last strains of music at midnight bade the dancers that "Home Sweet Home" was the grand finale of a great celebration.

At 2 o'clock in the afternoon the guests were ushered into the dining room which had been transformed into a bower of beauty. Every inch of wall space was hidden with huge brake ferns through which streamers of red, white and blue were gracefully entwined. The center of attraction was the table with seating capacity for sixty and never have I seen a more beautiful sight. The decorations consisted of stands of sweet peas of the national colors while a beautiful center piece was a skillful arrangement of small silk flags, maidenhair ferns and flowers. Over the table at intervals were suspended hanging baskets filled with different hued dahlias. The effect was gorgeous and the credit of it all belongs to Messrs. Chas. L. Pioda, Bob Ford, Paul Pioda and Sargeant Schen.

Then the eats! My; but what we had—all sorts of salads, ch tongue, ham, fruits, cakes, candy, nuts and last, but not least, a punch that had an enormous amount of kick in it. Chas. L. Pioda occupied the seat at the head of the table as toast-master. Mrs. Quilty made a wise selection, as Mr. Pioda proved very capable, not only making a fine address himself but inducing others to follow suit, so that wit and laughter flowed with the punch. At the close of the banquet which occupied two hours, everyone stood and joined in singing "America."

At 5 o'clock the races took place—potato, egg, sack, and three-legged, and much amusement was afforded. Little Bill and Jim Jeffery entered in nearly every contest and won first money many times.

Last week we had a mock divorce trial that caused great fun. Mr. Pioda was the all-just and all-wise judge, and after hearing the testimony of many witnesses and arguments of the able counsel—Professor D. C. Ahlers of Santa Cruz and Sergeant Otto Schen, U. S. A., the verdict was that the parties be condemned to live together in perfect connubial bliss for the rest of their lives.

Today there was a great barbecue. Tables were set under famous old Gossip oak, and steaks broiled to perfection by Dan Leddy of Watsonville and Pete Wallace of Salinas. Bob Ford made the salad and helped in every capacity at once, so you know how "quiet" things were. Fifty-four were seated and about half through eating when an automobile arrived with five guests. A few minutes afterward two wagon loads of campers added to the crowd, and three government men came in on horseback, but there was plenty to eat for all. There are three by Mr. Wm. Hatton of Monterey, one by Bill Rhyner of Spreckels and one by Jim Okseh of Watsonville. Deer is very plentiful this year everywhere.

Mr. and Mrs. Chas. Bardin arrived Friday.

Mutt is one of the principal card games and at any time a game is easy to get.

The weather is very delightful this year, being neither hot nor cold. Will send another budget soon.

MESCAL.

Salinas Daily Index, July 16, 1914
Photo top right—dining room, July 4, 1914
[Read transcription in Appendix p. 160.]

Group dining under Gossip Oak, c. 1915

Club House, c. 1915

Tassajara Hotel, c. 1915

Dining under Gossip Oak, c. 1917

Tassajara Hot Springs
California's Greatest Natural Wonder

Postcard, c. 1915

Card small print reads: Located in Monterey County, in the U.S. Forest Reserve. Altitude 1750 feet [1637]. There is a Sandstone Hotel, numerous Hot Springs, Sulphur plunges, Tiled and Porcelain Tubs, Steam Bath over Boiling Spring, Fine Trout Fishing, Deer Hunting, Dancing, Bowling, Billiards, Club. ... Owner gives personal attention to management. Excellent Table, Comfortable Beds, Legendary Surroundings. Guests return every season. Post Office, Telephone, Telegraph.

Gossip Oak, c. 1918

Many's a time I've stretched out in that hammock and listened to the gossip with Gossip Oak. —Helen Scherrer

There were two large old trees in front of the dining room, a sycamore and an oak. It was shady under the trees, with a bit of a breeze, and they were centrally located so a person could keep track of what was going on with everyone at all times. Sometimes eight or ten people were in the hammock at once. There was a flat rock in the retaining wall that Helen Quilty sat on every afternoon so she could share in the gossip. Ira Bailey recalled, "Gossip Oak was full of grey squirrels. In the mornin' there was the most awful uproar 'cause the blue jays roosted there too. There was always a row between the squirrels and the jays. People would sit around under the trees and watch 'em perform."

In 1889, someone painted an Indian chief on a rock in the stream bed below the barn. They named him Old Tass. The rock is no longer there.

Old Tass, c. 1910

Maiden, c. 1930

Helen Quilty thought it would be fun if they also had the head of an Indian maiden. In 1918, Harrison Fisher, a well-known artist of the day, offered to paint the picture. With the help of friends, Helen Quilty worked out the Legend of Tassajara.

During one of the annual pilgrimages of the coast tribes to Tassajara, which they made unfailingly for the benefits of the curative waters, a young Indian girl named Chanta Seechee fled from her father's teepee with a warrior from a hostile tribe. Her fiancé followed the couple and as they reached the rocks where the picture of the maiden is painted, overtook and killed them both.

Quilty organized a contest to find a model. Mary Harkins had black hair and looked a bit like an Indian. Fisher painted her likeness on a rock a short way up the road. Although faded, it can be seen today.

Mary Harkins, Harrison Fisher, 1918

Indian Maiden and hikers, c. 1925

Helen Quilty was a very outgoing, fun-loving person and she thrived on a good party. She planned dances, minstrel shows, card games, masquerades, poetry readings, croquet, horseshoes, hikes, and costume parties with prizes for the winners. There was always something to do.

Under Mrs. Quilty you didn't dare say there was a snake around here. I killed one right at her backdoor. "Shhh," she said. "Don't say anything. It'll scare all the guests away and we won' ever get them back in here again."
—Paul Clinefelter

Mrs. Quilty ruled Tassajara with an iron hand. —Ira Bailey

She use'ta drink. Thought nobody knew it too. But I'd been drinkin' since I was a young boy, and I could sure tell.
—Bill Lambert

Helen Quilty, c. 1925

She always wore a corset, high-laced shoes, and long dresses.   —Bill Lambert

The dance platform, built in 1899, was a special favorite with the guests. In 1902 Bill Jeffery planted mountain maple trees around the platform. Helen Quilty would often hire a dance band, and the guests would dance late into the night.

One time I was up there and they were havin' a dance and the spring broke on the phonograph and I spent all night twirlin' the darn phonograph with my fingers so the dancin' could go on. —Charles William Jeffery

Any kinda' opportunity for a celebration, she'd have one—to relieve the monotony. Everybody'd get up there on that platform and dance. —Ella Enevoldsen

Dance Platform, c. 1930

From their earliest times at the Springs, guests loved to hike. They called it "going on a tramp." Helen Quilty would have Sam the cook make up special lunches for the hikers. On opening weekend in May, there would be a race to Flag Rock to see who could place the flag first, and then there would be a prize for the winner. In the early 1920s Quilty had a register placed at the top of Flag Rock so the hikers could sign in.

As far as amusements were concerned in those days, you just sort of made up your own. Almost every day we had hikes somewhere. It would take up the whole day. When we came back we'd take the baths.
—Paul Pioda

Flag Rock, c. 1910

On a hike, c. 1910

In the early days, the women stayed dressed up. The men would always have stockings and shoes, never shorts or sports type clothes. The women didn't show their ankles ever.
—Anonymous

In the creek, c. 1915

Before Helen Quilty had a swimming pool constructed in 1920, there were swimming holes both upstream and downstream. The rocks would be moved from the stream bed early in the spring so there would be a deep hole for diving and swimming.

Years ago, if the boys wanted a plunge in the cold water they'd go on down the creek. One time another fella and I dressed up in Mrs. Quilty's clothes and went on down and surprised the boys. They were all down there and had forgot their bathin' suits. —Paul Pioda

The Narrows, c. 1919

The swimming pool was finished in time for the beginning of the 1921 season. The same pool is still in use today. It is thirty feet wide by sixty feet long and from three to eight feet deep. Cold stream water and hot spring water are combined and piped to the pool. The water constantly runs out an exit pipe, and therefore no chemicals or filtering equipment are necessary. The opening of the swimming pool was a major event, and the *Watsonville Pajaronian* made this report in April 1921:

Swimming pool opens, May 1921

The matter of suitable bathing suits for the swimming tank, that is, the selection of something that would be appropriate and attractive having been left to the Pajaronian Editor, we have advised Mrs. Quilty to write to Paris for some of the Seymour designs, said to be the greatest ever. They are very chic, and calculated to make the swim tank the most popular place at the Springs.

Stylish swimsuits, c. 1930

Playing cards was a favorite pastime. There were bridge games that lasted for days and poker games that continued late into the night. Many of the guests played horseshoes in the driveway across from the hotel, or played croquet, or rode the horses. There was never a problem finding something to do. Including fishing on Tassajara Creek.

c. 1915

c. 1930

My brother went to Tassajara every year for fifty-four consecutive years on the first day of fishing season. —Rose Rhyner

W.J. Rhyner, May 1960

Fishing is keen sport and not much work, as the creek is full of trout. It being possible to throw a line from the dining room window, catch a shining beauty, throw it through the kitchen window to Sunny Jim, the cook, who will soon serve it hot and brown and garnished with curling parsley, a toothsome dainty to whet the weakest appetite.
—*Salinas Weekly Index*, 1911

Early Tassajara was paradise for hunters and fishermen. One old-timer remembered catching one hundred ten fish in five hours. By the mid-1920s fish had become seriously depleted in Tassajara Creek. In July 1925 thirty-five thousand young rainbow trout were planted by the government to replenish streams in the Santa Lucia Mountains, but they were soon fished out. By the late 1930s the abundance of trout in Tassajara Creek was over.

Hallock, he drove the horse stage for many years. He use'ta play tricks on the hunters in Tassajara. Whenever any of the hunters was goin' out with him, he'd always see a big buck deer the evening before when he was comin' in. So the hunters would walk up, lookin' for the buck, and that'd be lighter on his team goin' up the grade. —Paul Pioda

Unknown hunter, c. 1898

Lilian Victorine, on horse with rifle, deer and hunting dog, c. 1910

July Fourth was a big day at Tassajara. People came from the surrounding ranches and joined the Tassajara guests in the festivities. There were fireworks, a barbeque, often a masquerade, and always a wonderful party.

We had many a good time at Tassajara, I can tell you that. —Anonymous

Fourth of July celebrations at Tassajara, c. 1920

Coal oil lamps provided lighting at the Springs in the early days. Later, gas mantle lamps were installed around the hotel and along the walkways. Around 1920 Helen Quilty had a small power plant installed that was used mainly for refrigeration. In May 1924 the *Watsonville Pajaronian* reported this about a new lighting system:

> Residents of the Santa Lucia Mountain sections, southwest of here, as well as those traveling through the mountains, thought they were witnessing a rare phenomenon last night when Tassajara Springs was illuminated for the first time by electricity. When the juice was switched on, more than one thousand incandescent lamps sent up a blaze of light, that from a distance looked like a huge ball of fire surrounded by an arc. Many mistook it for that wonderful natural display, the aurora borealis.... Mrs. Helen Quilty, proprietress of the Springs, has recently had the lighting system installed at an expense of more than five thousand dollars. The plant consists of a generator set, operated by a thirty-five horsepower Waukesha four cylinder gasoline engine, as well as a storage battery system. On its initial trial it was found to work perfectly.

Helen Quilty had a difficult time finding people willing to work at Tassajara. All stage drivers had instructions to give new employees a wild ride to the Springs, to scare them into staying. Most workers were hired in San Jose or San Francisco. All kitchen workers were Chinese males. Maids and waitresses were middle-aged white women. There was also a barber, the hunter-handyman, a gardener, a bell-hop, and a masseuse and masseur.

Plotnekoff was a Russian. Don't know if he was a real doctor or not, but everybody called him Doc. He had arms like a football player. First you went in the plunges and when you were bright red you went upstairs and the Doc would wrap you in wool blankets and let you sweat. While he gave a massage he'd sing, "If I had a thousand lives to live, I'd live them all for you." I've seen them get out of a wheelchair up there and in just a few days they were walkin'. He'd always say, "Take a hot bath and I'll fix you."

—Paul Pioda

Doc Plotnekoff, c. 1917

All staff, 1917

Two of the girls was waitresses. One was the chambermaid. One man was the barber, other was the gardener. I'm the one on the left. I did everything. Washed dishes, peeled potatoes, carried baggage, cleaned fish, got sulphur water for the guests. You name it, I did it. Made lot more money in tips than I did in wages. —Harry Koue

Mrs. Quilty'd put on her Irish brogue and have great talks with Coffee, the hunter-handyman. After they'd had a few drinks, they'd get to fightin'. Then Coffee'd sit down at the piano and play "Mother McCree" and Mrs. Quilty would cry. —Ira Bailey

Coffee with rifle and dog, c. 1917

This man, he invented paperclips. Just ordinary paperclips. He got ten thousand dollars a year for the patent rights. That was a fabulous fortune in those days. He'd work all day long makin' pincushions out of yucca stalk. We called it mescal. He had a bunch of wire and some tin snips and pliers and he'd be sittin' there makin' pincushions all day long. —Ira Bailey

Kenneth Vanderhurst, c. 1923

When the county widened the road and eliminated the worst part of Tony's Boulevard in the early 1920s, Ira Bailey knew his stage line would soon be in direct competition with people driving their own cars to Tassajara. In 1923 he gave up his contract with Helen Quilty and retired from the auto stage business. Bailey said, "In the eight years I had the stage line, and with all the people I hauled and all the drivers I had, we never had an accident of any kind. I think that's quite a record."

Bailey sold his Salinas-based livery business to Kenneth Vanderhurst and Al Duda. They kept the stage line running to Tassajara until the late 1920s, when they sold it to Bruce Robb. By the mid-1930s people drove their own cars to the Springs, and there was no longer a need for a stage line.

Between 1920 and 1930 Tassajara became much less a health spa and much more a resort. An automobile in every family gave people mobility they had not had before, and this changed Tassajara substantially. People no longer went to the Springs for three weeks or a month; now they could drive in from Carmel and Salinas for dinner, or just to stay overnight.

July 4th, 1920

Mrs. Quilty never allowed two cars on the Tassajara Road at the same time. —Ira Bailey

Tassajara Road, c. 1920

The Cascades, c. 1920

Tassajara Road, c. 1930

That's what ruined Tassajara for the old-timers, the advent of the automobile. When they rode in on the horse stage, they had to stay two or three weeks in order to recuperate for the ride out. Automobiles changed that. —Ira Bailey

From 1919, when the Volstead Act was passed and prohibition started, until 1933, when it was repealed, Helen Quilty closed the Club House as a bar and used it as a card room and barber shop—with no liquor served. Guests brought bootleg liquor and drank it in their rooms.

Prohibition made cheaters outa' everybody. We all drank. —Bill Lambert

People went up to the Flats to drink. They'd have parties at night. Mrs. Quilty didn't like it, but they did it anyway. —Paul Pioda

Club House, c. 1932

During bootleg days my dad was alive. Mrs. Quilty always liked my father, and when she wanted to go in there she'd make arrangements with my dad and he'd drive her in. Dad always took a two-gallon barrel of whiskey with him. She'd say, "Bill, I think it's about time we stopped here. Better have a little sip of that whiskey." So they'd pull the plug and have a little drink. Right out of the barrel. —Bill Lambert

During the early 1920s William "Pat" Foster (left) moved to Jamesburg. He ran the post office, the open-air dance pavilion, and the soft drink stand for about thirty years. An ex-fighter and ex-boilermaker from San Francisco, he was known as the Mayor of Jamesburg. Foster, as everyone called him, sold home-brewed beer and cold drinks to people en route to the Springs. He loved to play practical jokes on his patrons. Foster would ask, "You wanna' call Tassajara Hot Springs?" Then he would give the person a telephone that wasn't connected to anything. He owned the last slot machine in the county.

They use'ta come from far and wide to see him. He was a real character. —Anonymous

He had the best home brew in the country. He was a charmer. If Foster had a goat hide hanging over the fence, that was the signal that he had killed a deer out of season and it was being served for dinner. —Richard Lamb

He once taped a medicine ball to a tree and passed it off as the world's largest apple, developed by a new scientific serum. Visitors faithfully took pictures by the hundreds.
—Bill Lambert

I bit on everything that he had going. He was a real wisecracker. He use'ta get plastered—they all did then, those mountain people. And of course you know those mountain people lie. They think it's cute. That's just a joke among them. —Anna Beck

In July 1927, because of her desire to retire, Helen Quilty left Tassajara. A group of Salinas businessmen, under the name Tassajara Hot Springs Company, leased or rented the Springs, probably with an option to buy.

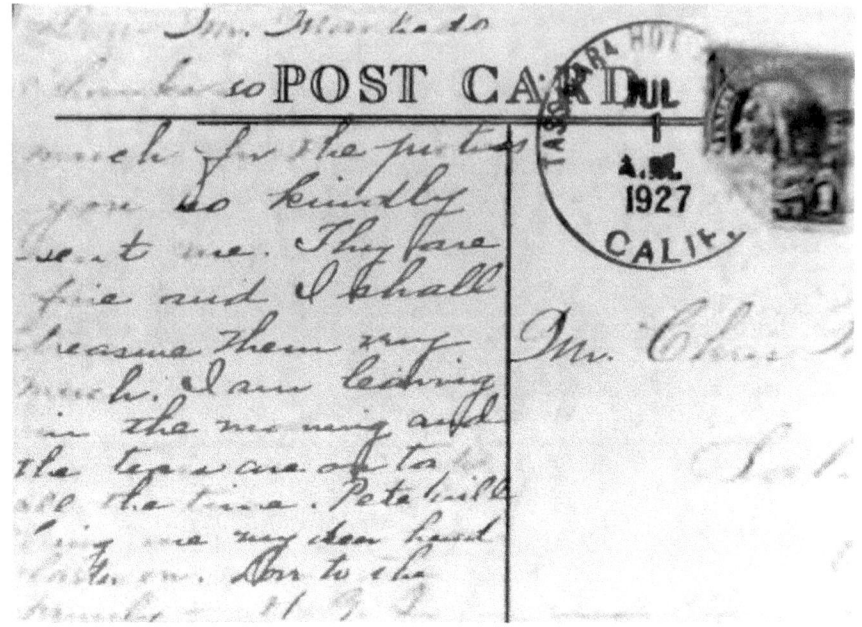

Postcard sent by Helen Quilty the day she left Tassajara
Note Tassajara Hot Springs postmark.

Postcard reads:

Dear Mr. Machado, Thanks so much for the pictures you so kindly sent me. They are fine and I shall treasure them very much. I am leaving in the morning and the tears are on tap all the time. Pete will bring my deer head later on. Love to the Family—HGQ

The Tassajara Hot Springs Company hired George Kingsbury as manager and put Mrs. Kingsbury in charge of the dining room. On September 15, 1927, they closed Tassajara in order to make extensive improvements before winter came. Six private bathtub rooms were added on the front of the plunges, and enlarged quarters for the masseuse and masseur were constructed upstairs. They built a twenty-thousand-gallon reservoir up the road and a concrete steam room over the springs in the stream bed. The road was widened in twenty-four places. All the buildings were freshly painted. A new manager, I.J. Cornett, opened Tassajara for the season in May 1928.

Plunges with six private bathtub rooms, c. 1928

The minerals in the water ruined those new bathtubs. They got all discolored right away.
—Paul Clinefelter

The Baths, c. 1930

SONGS of CALIFORNIA
by Miles Overholt

TASSAJARA

There's a town in the mountains whose name will endure—
"A-place-where-jerked-meat-is-hung-up-to-cure!"
And here are some springs full of mineral wealth
That people there tell you will bring you new health.
The name, Tassajara, is short, to be sure,
For "A-place-where-jerked-meat-is-hung-up-to-cure!"

A lot of these names may be viewed with alarm,
But that is a part of this glory state's charm,
Though one sometimes halts with a wondering frown
When he thinks of the name he is calling a town!
But here is a place where all things must be pure—
"A-place-where-jerked-meat-is-hung-up-to-cure!"

San Francisco Chronicle—January 19, 1930

Yucca above Tassajara

I've measured them almost twenty feet high. I've measured growth of nineteen inches in twenty-four hours. You could almost see them grow. —Ira Bailey

The Cabins in snow, c. 1928

Hotel with snow, c. 1930

Helen Quilty, believing she was free of all responsibility at Tassajara, married James Holohan in February 1931. Holohan had been a state senator, U.S. marshal, and sheriff of Santa Cruz County. In September 1927 he was appointed warden of San Quentin Prison. After the wedding Helen Quilty moved into the warden's house on the grounds at San Quentin.

The stock market crash of 1929, and the Great Depression that followed, had a severe effect on the resort business. Mrs. Quilty-Holohan, as she was now called, had to repossess Tassajara in the fall of 1932. Malcolm and Irene Laird, who had been working at the Springs for a year as caretakers, were hired to stay on year-round.

Mrs. Quilty-Holohan was lucky when she took Tassajara back because it had been kept in such good condition. —Irene Laird

Salinas Index-Journal, **July 1933**
(text below)

Where are you going to spend your vacation this summer? At Tassajara Hot Springs, of course. Because the mineral waters are as hot and beneficial as ever—the climate as wonderful—the table as good and wholesome—and because the owner and manager for many years—Mrs. Helen G. Quilty-Holohan is returning to again cater to the comfort and amusements of the guests. Rates reduced to suit the times. Write for information or get folders at Index-Journal.

In 1932, there were two Pierce Arrow stages. One seated eleven, the other seated nine. They drove round-trip to the Springs every day. The stage left Salinas or Tassajara at seven a.m. and was back by five p.m. The stage driver hauled the laundry and the groceries. There were three stage drivers during the 1930s: Svend Kraul, Malcolm Laird, and Bruce Robb.

Svend Kraul driving the stage, c. 1932

Malcom Laird and the stage, c. 1933

TASSAJARA STAGES
Tassajara Hot Springs, Calif.
AUTO BUS
PASSENGER TIME TABLE NO. 5
Cancelling Time Table No. 4

Issued May 1, 1937 - Effective May 17, 1937

SALINAS TO TASSAJARA				TASSAJARA TO SALINAS			
Station	Arrive	Leave	Fare	Station	Arrive	Leave	Fare
SALINAS		1:00 P. M.		TASSAJARA		7:00 A. M.	
JUNCTION	1:20 P. M.		$ .50	CHINA CAMP	7:50 A. M.		$1.25
RANCHO DEL MONTE	1:40 P. M.		1.00	SUMMIT CHEWS RIDGE	8:00 A. M.		1.50
CAMP STEFFANI	1:50 P. M.		1.25	BRUCE RANCH	8:15 A. M.		2.25
CACHAGUA	2:05 P. M.		1.50	JAMESBURG	8:45 A. M.		3:00
JAMESBURG	2:40 P. M.	3:00 P. M.	2.00	CACHAGUA	9:10 A. M.		3.50
BRUCE RANCH	3:25 P. M.		2.75	CAMP STEFFANI	9:20 A. M.		3.75
SUMMIT CHEWS RIDGE	3:45 P. M.		3.50	RANCHO DEL MONTE	9:35 A. M.		4.00
CHINA CAMP	3:55 P. M.		3.75	JUNCTION	9:55 A. M.		4.50
TASSAJARA	4:30 P. M.		5.00	SALINAS	10:15 A. M.		5.00
		Round Trip, $8.00				Round Trip, $8.00	

PACKAGES AND FREIGHT SHOULD BE LEFT AT HOTEL JEFFERY
NOT LATER THAN 12:00 NOON

Terminals: HOTEL JEFFERY, Salinas
TASSAJARA HOT SPRINGS

Issued by
B. W. ROBB
Salinas, California

Bruce Robb and stage, 1938

Bruce Robb bought one or two buses from a millionaire who had had them built extra-long so he could haul all his friends to the duck club. —Irene Laird

They drove those stages so fast through my yard, nothin' I did would slow them down. So, I dug two ditches across the road. When Robb hit 'em it just broke the stage right in two. —Bill Lambert

Many of the guests at the Springs in the 1930s were second and third generation Tassajara devotees. The parents had come in the late 1800s and brought their children from the time they were little. A number of these children became successful businesspeople in Salinas, Watsonville, and Monterey. Tassajara was a great place to get away from business and relax.

Bridge to plunges, c. 1930

In 1936, it was mostly the lettuce crowd from Salinas. The men were in town most of the time because of the strike. A bunch of the women were out there at Tassajara. They'd get up in the morning and start drinkin'. In the afternoon, they'd go down to the spring and drink sulphur water 'til they threw up. Then they'd start drinkin' again. —Anonymous

Dining room, 1930

The Tassajara truck, c. 1930

Helen Quilty-Holohan installed a Lorimer diesel motor to supply electricity for refrigeration and lighting. It replaced the motor that had been in operation since 1924. The base the motor sat on was seven and a half tons of concrete, and the flywheel weighed eight hundred and fifty pounds. To conserve power, the caretaker would switch from seventy-five-watt bulbs to twenty-five-watt bulbs on the pathways and in the restrooms at 11 p.m. every night. The guests had instructions to turn out all lights by 10 p.m.

Lorimer Diesel Engine, c. 1938

It ran all day long. Boom, boom, boom. I use'ta be up on Flag Rock and it would sound like a foundry down there 'cause of the echo out of the valley.
—Paul Clinefelter

In the late 1930s Quilty-Holohan decided to build a new bar. She planned a very dramatic structure that spanned the creek, but settled for a more economical building when she found out what it would cost to build the fancy one.

Pine bar room and bar porch, c. 1947

In January 1935 Warden Holohan was severely beaten when he tried to stop four prisoners attempting an escape from San Quentin. He resigned as warden in April 1936. He was state senator from 1940 through 1947 and lived mainly in Watsonville. Helen Quilty-Holohan joined him there when she closed Tassajara for the winter, from October until May.

She use'ta have what was called the Command Post at the back of the hotel. Holohan was warden at San Quentin. She was warden at Tassajara. —Bill Lambert

In 1942 because of World War II, the lack of manpower, and the chance of fire, the government closed the Los Padres National Forest. Shortly after that, gas rationing and the unavailability of food forced Quilty-Holohan to close Tassajara. She moved to a suite in the Resetar Hotel in Watsonville with Holohan.

Helen Quilty, c. 1935

On October 29, 1947, Helen Quilty-Holohan died. She had owned Tassajara for almost forty years and was, without a doubt, one of the most popular landladies who ever presided over a California resort.

In May 1945 Ralph "Cocky" Myers and James Bundgard bought Tassajara from Helen Quilty-Holohan. Myers had worked at the Springs as a lifeguard and maintenance man while he was going to school, and he knew Quilty-Holohan well. At the time of the purchase, he was the owner of a large growing, packing, and shipping company in Salinas. During World War II he taught recruits to fly. His interest in planes was carried over to his produce business. He shipped the first strawberries by air from Salinas to the Waldorf Astoria Hotel in New York City. He was also one of the first people to ship produce by air all over the U.S.

Ralph Myers, c. 1945

Myers's partner, James Bundgard, leased his share in the Springs to Myers, who wanted to develop Tassajara into an exclusive resort. He planned to bulldoze the hill behind the plunges and build a helicopter landing pad with a tram car that would cross the stream and bring the passengers safely and smoothly to the door of the hotel. He also planned to initiate a helicopter shuttle service from the city to Tassajara and try to gain the interest of San Francisco businessmen. Another idea Myers had was to build the road from the Springs downstream to Arroyo Seco, as originally developed by Charles Quilty in 1904.

Mrs. Myers recalled:

> I had never seen Tassajara. The first time I went was about two months after my daughter was born. There were some friends there, about ten or twelve of them. I looked at the place. It was a mess, filthy. I thought, dear God, now what has Ralph done. I've never in my life seen such a horrible place. But you know, I stayed there for about a week and then I went home and I could hardly wait 'til I got back there. It gets under your skin. I really loved Tassajara.

Ralph and Helen Myers didn't open Tassajara to the public the first year they owned it. Friends and business acquaintances were invited for weekend parties. Ralph Myers would bring half a side of beef or some large pork roasts and crates of vegetables, and Helen Myers and Mrs. Bundgard would cook for the guests. There were poker games, lots of drinking, and everyone had a wonderful time.

Pajama Lane, c. 1947

When Cocky owned it, there was twelve thousand dollars on the table in one poker game. You'd go up there and drink and lay by the pool and you'd fish and you'd eat. It was such a super place you didn't want to do anything. —Anonymous

The Club House, c. 1947

Cocky Myers was a character and that's all there was to it. He lived up to the name Cocky—he was so sure of himself. —Bill Lambert

The first time I ever rode in a car over 100 mph was with Cocky. —Anonymous

In May 1946 Ralph and Helen Myers opened Tassajara to the public with Elmer and Sybil Faul as managers. Tragically, in returning from a polo match in San Mateo on June 16, 1946, Ralph Myers's private airplane crashed, killing him and the pilot, Phillip Prader.

Flowers were sent to the cemetery for six weeks after the funeral. A lot of people loved him.
—Helen Myers

Guests, c. 1947

In 1947 Helen Myers decided to open the Springs on her own. She started to remodel and update the old buildings at Tassajara. She recalled, "I'd start working at 6 a.m. and get to bed at 1 or 1:30 in the morning. I took a nap every afternoon. I'd call the telephone company and say, 'I'm gonna' have my nap now, so don't put through any calls to Tassajara until I call you back.'"

In the hotel, she added a bathroom for every room, put in new wiring and plumbing, added a new asbestos shingle roof, and bought new carpet, new mattresses, and wool blankets for all the beds. The lobby was decorated with big leather armchairs, thick rugs, and beautiful lamps.

Helen Myers had the interior and exterior of the Club House, dining room, and the stone bathhouse buildings sandblasted, restoring them to their original rock.

All the cabins were painted inside and out. The front would be bright yellow, the sides orange or blue, each side a different color.

Hotel, c. 1947

Helen Myers, c. 1947

Cabins, c. 1947

With Australian plane trees planted in the 1930s

Cabin interior, c. 1947

The remodeling was finished and Helen Myers reopened the resort in May 1949. In June, she married Phillip Terry, a movie actor. Together they managed Tassajara.

He made a great hotelman 'cause he loved to talk to people. —Mr. Mehne

He always liked to sit underneath Gossip Oak and chat with the guests.
—Anonymous

Phillip Terry, c. 1949

A brochure from 1949

On September 9, 1949, a fire started in the cabin that was used by Helen Myers-Terry as a nursery for the three Myers children. Although there are many versions of the origin of the fire, the truth still remains a mystery. The flames went from the cabin to the treetops and then to the eaves of the hotel, which burned for four days. There were forty guests and twenty-two employees present and everyone pitched in to fight the blaze. No one was seriously injured.

First report of the fire from a teletype printout, September 9, 1949

```
1ST LEAD FIRE
          BY WALTER BARKDULL
                 UNITED PRESS STAFF CORRESPONDENT
   KING CITY, CALIF., SEPT 9-(UP) SIXTY-TWO GUESTS AND
EMPLOYEES OF SWANK TASSAJARA HOT SPRINGS RESORT WON A BATTLE
FOR THEIR LIVES IN SIX FEARFUL HOURS LAST NIGHT WHEN A
BURNING CABIN MUSHROOMED IN-TO A FOREST FIRE DEATH TRAP.
THE FIRE CONTINUED TO RAGE OUT OF CONTROL NEAR THE SANTA
LUCIA MOUNTAIN RESORT TODAY BUT THE 62 COURAGEOUS MEN,
WOMEN AND CHILDREN WERE SAFE, THANKS TO THEIR
OWN BRAVE EFFORTS.
   AT DAWN, U. S. FOREST SERVICE RANGERS SAID THE WIND-
WHIPPED FIRE FRONT HAD BURNED OVER THE CREST OF NEARBY BLACK
BUTTE MOUNTAIN DESPITE THE EFFORTS OF MORE THAN 500 FIRE
FIGHTERS·
   IN ITS WAKE WERE MORE THAN 1,200 ACRES OF BLACKENED OAK
AND BRUSH LAND, INCLUDING THE SMOULDERING REMAINS OF THE
RESORT'S 36 ROOM HOTEL, NINE CABINS, A LARGE RECREATION
HALL, A 20-CAR GARAGE AND A REPAIR SHOP.
   THE FIRE, WHICH BROKE OUT LATE YESTERDAY AFTERNOON IN
THE CABIN OF RESORT OWNER PHILIP TERRY, FANNED OUT LIKE A
PRAIRIE BLAZE, CUTTING OFF THE OCCUPANTS' ESCAPE ROUTE AND
SEVERING COMMUNICATIONS. THE FATE OF THE TRAPPED PEOPLE WAS
UNKNOWN FOR MORE THAN SIX HOURS AND IT WAS FEARED THEY HAD
ROASTED ALIVE IN THE FIERY TRAP. IT WASN'T UNTIL 9 P.M. LAST
NIGHT THAT TWO HEROIC RANGERS DASHED THROUGH A VERITABLE
TUNNEL OF FLAME TO REACH THE RESORT.
   DISTRICT RANGER GEORGE BRANAGH, WHO MADE THE TORTUOUS
TRIP WITH FIRE CONTROL OFFICER JACK CURRAN, REPORTED
OVER HIS PORTABLE RTADIO THAT "ALL WERE SAFE".
   OWNER TERRY, EX-ACTOR AND FORMER HUSBAND OF SCREEN
STAR JOAN CRAWFORD, WAS THE FIRST TO REACH THE STRANDED
RESORT. FEARFUL FOR THE SAFETY OF HIS WIFE, HELEN, AND
THREE CHILDREN, HE RACED TO THE FIRE AREA FROM NEARBY
SALINAS, DASHING THE LAST MILE ON FOOT AFTER HE WAS
FORCED TO ABANDON HIS CAR AT A BURNED OUT BRIDGE.
   HIS AUTOMOBILE WAS COMPLETELY DESTROYED BY THE WALL
OF FIRE THAT SWEPT ACROSS THE ROAD SHORTLY AFTER HE
PASSED THROUGH.
   THIS CORRESPONDENDT REACHED THE HOT SPRINGS SHORTLY
AFTER DAWN TO FIND THE 62 GUESTS AND RESORT WORKERS
SMOKE-BLACKENED AND EXHAUSTED, BUT HAPPY TO BE ALIVE.
```

THEY SAID THE FIRE BROKE OUT IN TERRY'S CABIN ABOUT 3 P. M., SHORTLY AFTER HIS CHILDREN, MICHAEL 8, EDWIN, 6, AND MARY 5, HAD LEFT TO GO SWIMMING. MRS. HELEN TERRY SUFFERED A BURNED ARM WHEN SHE ATTEMPTED TO ENTER THE BURNING CABIN THINKING THE CHILDREN WERE STILL INSIDE. RESORT EMPLOYEE CHARLES RONSON SUFFERED A BURNED HAND.

RANGERS AT THE RESORT HAD HIGH PRAISE FOR HOTEL ROOM CLERK BERT PLUMP WHO QUICKLY ORGANIZED THE 40 GUESTS AND 22 EMPLOYEES INTO A FIRE FIGHTING UNIT.

MEN, WOMEN AND CHILDREN GRABBED UP WATER BUCKETS, SHOVELS AND AXES AND PITCHED IN BUILDING FIRE BREAKS AND SPRINKLING THE ROOFS OF UNBURNED BUILDINGS TO PREVENET THE SPREAD OF FLAMES. THERE WAS NO PANIC OF ANY SORT.

LEO ROSS, MONTEREY, CA, SAID THE WOMEN GUESTS WERE "MARVELOUS".

"THEY TOOK BLANKETS AND WET CLOTHES AND REALLY PITCHED IN TO FIGHT THE FIRE" HE SAID. "IT WAS LIKE AN INFERNO".

PHILIP LILIENTHALN, HILLSBORO, CA CATTLEMAN, PRAISED THE ACTIONS OF MRS. TERRY.

"MRS. TERRY AND I TRIED TO PUT OUT THE FIRE IN THE FIRST CABIN BUT IT GOT AWAY FROM US. SHE WAS CALM, COLLECTED AND PERFECTLY MARVELOUS."

R. E. MEHNE, WATSONVILLE, SAID HE WAS TAKING A MID-AFTERNOON NAP IN HIS HOTEL ROOM WHEN THE FIRE STARTED AND HE WAS AWAKENED BY FELLOW GUESTS.

"I GRABBED MY CLOTHES AND A FEW THINGS AND RAN". HE RECALLED. THEN HE ADDED EMBARASSEDLY: "I GUESS I WAS EXCITED BECAUSE I RAN AROUND STRIPPED FOR ABOUT FIVE MINUTES BEFORE I THOUGHT TO PUT ON MY PANTS. THE FLAMES MOVED AROUND LIKE A BAT OUT OF HELL."

FOREST SERVICE MEN SAID THE GUESTS WOULD REMAIN AT THE RESORT UNTIL IT WAS CONSIDERED "SAFE" FOR THE WOMEN AND CHILDREN TO LEAVE. THEY POINTED OUT IT WAS A MILE OF ROUGH, SMOKING TRAIL TO THE NEAREST CLEAR ROAD AND SEVERAL "HOT SPOTS" BETWEEN THE RESORT AND THE ROAD PRESENTED A HAZARD. THE RESORT AREA ITSELF WAS NO LONGER CONSIDERED IN DANGER.

The bridges on Tassajara Road and the cabins across from the hotel were all burned in the first hour. Help from the convicts at Soledad Prison came about 3 a.m. The road was closed by the fire, and anyone coming to Tassajara had to hike.

Helen Quilty-Holohan had only carried ten thousand dollars insurance on Tassajara. Helen Myers-Terry had planned to increase that amount at the end of the 1949 season. It was almost a total loss. After that there would be no hotel at Tassajara, just more cabins.

The water tank burned right away. We had a hose, like you'd use to water the garden, but we couldn't do much with it. —Mr. Mehne

Someone had rescued a radio and we thought we'd listen to the news. They said there's a bad fire at Tassajara and it's believed all the people have perished. We heard that, and believe me it wasn't very encouraging. —Mr. Mehne

Hotel burning 1949

Mrs. Quilty-Holohan's dancing platform by the hotel burning, 1949

Mother had medicine she had to take—but I mean you didn't stop to think, I'm gonna' take this and take that. You just pushed it together and ran out. With burning embers falling on you, you weren't gonna' stand there and debate. I went back in and brought out one red shoe. Good thing I didn't go again, 'cause then the whole building collapsed.

—Robert Olsen

The burned hotel, 1949

We're standing in what's left of our hotel room. —Mr. Mehne

When things get really bad you either fall apart or you laugh about it. —Helen Myers-Terry

After the 1949 fire

It took four years to build it. Four days to burn it. Four hours to totally demolish it with a bulldozer. The intense heat from the fire caused cracks in the blocks and it had to be demolished. They pushed what remained into the basement and covered it with dirt.
—Helen Myers-Terry

The Terrys decided to open Tassajara again in 1950. Before the season they remodeled the stone bathhouse building, making it into family quarters for themselves. They built a fireplace, four bedrooms and two baths, and ran pipes under the cement floors for hot springs water to circulate and heat the rooms. They also remodeled the wooden portion of the dining room and it became the office and lobby.

Stone bathhouse as living quarters for the Terrys, c. 1950

Lobby and office, c. 1950

Tassajara reopened in May 1950. At the height of the season, there was a fire in the national forest. "For thirty days the ashes fell like snowflakes, totally blocking out the sun," Helen Myers-Terry recalled. Two fires in one year, coupled with the fact that the Myers children were of school age, helped them make the decision to sell the Springs.

Dining room, c. 1950

Cooks, c. 1950

You could always order as much as you wanted. One night a guest ordered six New York steaks. He was so proud of himself—that he was getting his money's worth. He was sick for two weeks after and couldn't eat a thing. —Helen Myers-Terry

There was a bell sitting on the ground near Gossip Oak that was said to be from the old Spreckels Railroad. It weighed between two and three hundred pounds. A guest welded it on a pole for use as a dinner bell.

Railroad Bell, c. 1950

Sunday buffet, c. 1950

Steam Room, c. 1950

Guests, c. 1950

We were thrilled it was open again and real curious to see how it was after all the remodeling she did. —Anonymous

The steam room was the most horrible thing you ever saw. Had green stuff all over the inside. The paint company said to leave it alone. We did as much as we could, but it only took a year and it was all green again.
—Helen Myers-Terry

When people come down, they always wanted to know—where was the road to go out. We just had to tell them—it's the same one you came in on.
—Helen Myers-Terry

Dining room, c. 1950

The Baths, c. 1950

We knocked our brains out maintaining it. A leaf would fall and someone'd rake it up.
—Helen Myers-Terry

Angela and Frank Sappok purchased Tassajara in October 1951. The Sappoks had come to the United States from Germany in 1929. They had worked in and owned hotels and a liquor store before buying the Springs. Under their ownership, Tassajara was a homey, relaxed resort. The food was excellent, the bar was congenial, and people enjoyed themselves.

Mom was the worker. She was the cook and a real great hostess too. But Dad, he was the host. To a certain degree, it was like being a con artist; he just knew how to schmooze the people. They liked it and he liked them and so that just worked out great.
—Hans Sappok

Angela and Frank Sappok, c. 1952

Angela Sappok ran the kitchen. She could take a chicken and make a substantial soup out of it to feed fifty people—and they would think a lot of everything went into it. She had been cooking for years, and had perfected her art when they owned the Franco Hotel in Castroville. The food was good and there was always plenty of it.

Dining room, c. 1952

A Brief History of Tassajara

As I recall, the guests were people who liked to drink a lot, eat a lot, and talk a lot.
—Anonymous

Best I ever been there when the Sappoks run it. They serve one of the finest foods they ever been served there. It was ten dollars a day. —Jack Novcich

Frank Sappok ran the bar. It was a rustic place, where everybody would get slightly loaded and tell outrageous stories. Frank Sappok wanted people to come to the bar to drink—not to stay in their rooms. When a guest would ask for ice he would give them a small child's sand bucket with a few ice cubes in it. He kept the room rates low and expected to make his money in the bar. He was noted for the jokes he told. One time he put a sawhorse in the corner of the barroom with a saddle draped over it for the amusement of his guests.

My husband had a few drinks and jumped on that saddle. "Put the saddle on the stove," he said. "I'm gonna' ride the range tonight." Just then he gave a mighty whoop, and he and the saddle fell to the floor. Luckily his injuries were minor. —Mrs. Shankle

The bar was a place where a lot of people went to just let down their hair. There was no danger of anyone sneaking in on them at Tassajara. —Anonymous

Bar, c. 1957

Dancing in the bar, c. 1957

They got more of the partying type of folks instead of the people who used to come and take the baths and rest. —Julie Levitt

Uranium Reported at Tassajara
SALINAS CALIFORNIAN

Salinas Californian, December 16, 1954

In December 1954 someone thought they discovered uranium at Tassajara. Richard Lamb, a Monterey businessman, said, "There are a lot of slate formations in the Santa Lucia Mountains and layers of slate secrete radon gasses which are highly radioactive. I worked over large areas of the mountains with a scintillator, a fancy Geiger counter, and found nothing but radon. No uranium."

The Sappoks, their daughter Dorothea, and their dog Lumpy lived at the Springs year-round. In April 1958 there was so much rain that the road was completely washed out and left them stranded. During the storm, the front part of the plunges was knocked off its foundation by the flooding creek. The bridges plugged up and the water flowed down the road into the stone buildings. The Army sent a helicopter with supplies, tools, and some friends who offered to help clean up the mess.

Tassajara Road after flood of April 1958

During the summer season of 1958, a young waitress, Annemarie Brunken, had been painting watercolors of different scenes around the Springs. Frank Sappok asked if she would paint a mural on the remaining wall of the plunges. Annemarie found a poem at the library that she used for the legend that accompanies the mural.

THE TASSAJARA HOT SPRINGS LEGEND

There once was an Indian chief, who was all powerful. He was the favorite of the Sun God that ruled the universe and from this deity received his powers. So supernatural was he that he could hear the grass grow and see his enemies and game a day's travel away. The chief had a young sister who was very dear to his heart and when she became stricken with a strange malady, the hills and dales were ransacked for herbs by the medicine man for a cure. Everything failing, the brother started her on a trip to the big water, hoping that the ocean would help her. By the time Tassajara Creek was reached the sister had failed so much that she could not go further. All powers of the chief had failed and her life was ebbing slowly. Finally in desperation he prayed to his Sun God, offering his own body as a sacrifice. He fell prone on the ground. Although it was mid-day the sun was soon obscured and the earth became dark. The body of the chief stiffened and he grew ridged and was turned to stone. As he dissolved into a mass of rock, hot tears poured forth. The sister fell prostrate over the sacrifice, and was soon covered with hot tears of her sorrowing brother. When she rose she was completely cured. The news of the miricale spread among the Indian tribes of California, and every year the lame, the halt and the blind wend their weary way to bathe in the hot waters which poured from the rock where the chief had died.

Legend of Tassajara on wall of the plunges, 1958
[See appendix p. 164 for transcription and more.]

In the 1950s, people were not as interested in spending their two-week vacation at Tassajara. They wanted to travel—have a vacation somewhere exotic like Tahoe, Las Vegas, or Hawaii. The Sappoks tried to run a resort that was only full on the weekends. During the week, there might be only fifteen or twenty guests. Keeping help was a problem. The Sappoks worked very hard but were never financially successful at Tassajara.

In November 1958 Frank Sappok went for a ride up the road in his jeep. He suffered a heart attack and the jeep overturned. He died from injuries sustained in this accident. Angela Sappok sold Tassajara the following year.

When the Hudsons—Margaret and Lester, well-to-do older people—bought the Springs in April 1959, they had no idea of the work that would be involved in running a resort as old and inaccessible as Tassajara. Margaret Hudson loved anything historical and thought Tassajara would be a nice thing for her husband, a retired admiral in the Navy, to putter with. Lester Hudson had allergies and low blood sugar, and was hard of hearing. He had had enough of people when he was in the Navy, and really was not at all interested in running a resort. The Hudsons hired managers to cover the daily business at the Springs. Both the admiral and his wife insisted on sleeping in their own bed, so at the end of the day they would drive back to Carmel. They never spent the night at Tassajara.

Admiral Lester Hudson and Margaret Hudson

They had a terrible problem keeping help. The bar ran out of ice constantly, and the telephone was always out of order. The Hudsons' son Tom, his wife Jane, and their family often had to assist with problems at the Springs. Bob Beck remembered this incident:

The stove there had come around the Horn on a sailing ship. It had been in the galley and worked on wood at one time. At Tassajara it was converted to stove oil. Had a big tank up high and the pressure was from the elevation of the tank. They had some kind of blower that made the oil vaporize to burn and that depended on water pressure. It was very complicated. If the water pressure went down the stove would go off and then it would explode. The first time we were there the breakfast was very slow, and finally the cook came out of the kitchen all covered with soot. He said, "Breakfast is going to be a little late—the stove just blew up again."

Tassajara proved to be too much work for the Hudson family. In February 1960, after only one season, they sold it to Robert and Anna Beck and Frederick and Nancy Roscoe. The Becks and the Roscoes had come to Tassajara as guests when the Hudsons owned it. Admiral Hudson wanted to sell the Springs and go home and relax. The Hudsons were very helpful with terms; all the admiral wanted was enough cash down to make a down payment on a Rolls Royce. Anna Beck sold her antique business in San Francisco, Robert resigned his teaching position, and the Roscoes put their respective San Francisco businesses up for sale. Robert remembered:

> We didn't have sense enough to know you didn't move to Tassajara in the winter on that road. In March 1960 Frederick and I started transporting great truckloads of our personal belongings and we immediately got stuck in the mud. One time the truck started sliding off the road—it was just chaos the whole time.

During the first month at Tassajara, the Roscoes changed their minds about being owners; their businesses weren't selling as expected, and Nancy discovered she was pregnant and didn't feel she would be able to do her fair share. In April the Becks bought the Roscoes' interest in Tassajara. Robert recalled:

> We had sold everything and I'd quit my job and there we were—in the resort business. Then we began to find out how really run-down the whole place was.

The buildings and equipment were in constant need of repair. Robert read "how-to" books. He and Anna built retaining walls, opened the baths to light and air by taking down the glass-brick wall across the front, and converted the pine barroom to guest rooms. In the stone bathhouse they installed showers, built terraces in the back, and put on a double-tiered roof to provide better drainage and make the rooms cooler. They created a lake above the baths by building a dam, part of which is still standing. The generator would break, the telephone was constantly out of order, and the water system was always in need of repair.

They pulled all the charm that was possible out of that place.
—Mrs. Hughes

It was a place that has so much appeal and so much draw, that many of us just kept going back. —Mrs. Yardell

Anna and Robert Beck, 1960

Anna was the decorator. She would put an old broken down pipe or something in a room and make it special. —David Walton

Lounge, 1962

Tassajara Hot Springs Resort

When the Hudsons bought the Springs, part of their bargain with Angela Sappok was that her dog, Lumpy, would stay. The Hudsons made the same agreement with the Becks. Lumpy became the official Tassajara greeter.

Lumpy's father was a Portagee dog from over near Jamesburg. —Bill Lambert

His name came from the German word that means "little bum." —Dorthea Howell

Lumpy, c. 1960

The Becks wanted to change the image at Tassajara. A friend advised, "You should do whatever you want to do to advertise, and in time the place will take on your character."

TASSAJARA SPRINGS An honestly out-of-the-ordinary old place in the mountains.

Our food, our waters, our climate and our guests are extraordinary.*

Possibly you too would like to relax in a somewhat different atmosphere.

Box 68   CARMEL VALLEY   PHONE TASSAJARA #1

*So is our road. (Actually one man called it an abomination, but he keeps coming back.)

Monterey Peninsula Herald, 1961 above & 1962 below

[more ads in Appendix p. 163]

TASSAJARA SPRINGS ... NOW OPEN ALL YEAR
TO ACCOMMODATE SMALL PARTIES AND INDIVIDUALS
Featuring off-season sports:
- Pine cone gathering
- Shove ha'penny
- Darts
- Leaf kicking
- Yucca hunting
- Bathing
- Wild boar talk

NOTE: If due to storminess in our mountains you are unable to return to your duties on time, we will write excuses.

P.O. BOX 68, CARMEL VALLEY, CALIFORNIA
PHONE: TASSAJARA SPRINGS NO. 1

Stand Still And Get Healthy

Charles McCabe

WED OCT 31 1962
Tassajara Hot Springs
Monterey County

San Francisco Chronicle

**Tassajara Hot Springs
Monterey County**

I took this battered body and tousled psyche down here for a spell to throw off the miasma created by the World Serious, the elfin play of the 49ers and Mr. Tittle of New York, and such strange eruptions in our State as those Brobdingnagians who now appear to be playing basketball for us.

This is a land of hot waters and cold airs guaranteed to irrigate the most sluggish of souls. It's only about two hours' drive from Monterey, but once here you're on a nepenthe jag.

As you perhaps know, I take a murky view of muscle-flexing, President Kennedy's fitness program (or anybody else's) and biceps nuts in general. I have no objection to feeling fit, but I hate working at it. If you're one of those people who want to feel like a tiger while doing nothing more strenuous than standing up, then Tassajara Hot Springs is your dish of tea.

"A spa for schemers and thinkers," is the way Bob and Anna Beck bill their Baden for battered psyches and physiques.

The general public is admitted, if they have Bohemian references. Athletics supporters are encouraged to take their custom elsewhere, like the nearest locker room.

"What we try to offer is an incomparable opportunity to get the city out of your system," says Bob. "The mellow atmosphere has been an honest 80 years in the making."

The Becks offer wood stoves, a mahogany bar, wine with meals, sycamore trees, badminton, cold nights, good conversation, hunting for deer, wild Russian boar, quail and wild pigeon in person. Also fishing for trout and carrier pigeons to keep in contact with civilization when the road goes out or when everybody is snowed in.

Tassajara, a true cul-de-sac, is at the end of what must be the worst passable auto road in California or maybe in the world. I drove in with an expert on lousy roads on several continents.

"This," she pronounced in the middle of the journey from Carmel Valley, "Is the cake-taker."

The real point of the thing is the mineral waters, in which you simply stand erect and become ten feet tall. The waters—plunges, vapor baths and chilling creek—contain sulphur, iron, soda, magnesium and the rare mineral lithium. These cure the tired body and, as they say, relax the tensions of modern-day living. The ladies say four minutes in the local Sulphur is worth a day at Helena Rubinstein's.

Career drinkers say the waters are the greatest known cure for a hangover, whether remote or proximate. That is, whether the indulgence was last night, or six months in a barroom. These experts further state the waters are even better than an ice-cold Coke before breakfast, a nostrum favored by Toots Shor and other ace tosspots.

Like all good spas, the spa for schemers has its own legend.

[McCabe repeats the legend on p. 119 word for word.]

This is such a good legend that Anna and Bob are thinking of getting a committee of three thinkers or so to authenticate it. Actually the legend sprang full-blown, like Minerva from the brow of Jupiter, from the inventive brain of a waitress in 1918. She suitably inscribed it above a painting outside the men's plunge.

I, for one, hope this legend makes it.

[McCabe was wrong about the legend source. It is rooted in Esselen lore. See pp. 118-119 and Appendix p. 164 for more on this legend including transcription.]

Robert Beck, c. 1962

In 1964 with the help of a good friend, Robert Beck moved three cabins from below the bridge to a new sunny position on Hotel Flat. They jacked them up, put them on rollers, and moved them with a jeep. Robert wanted to run water to them and knew that there was a water line somewhere up on the flat. He dug at the corner of a cabin, and not only found water, but had dug exactly where there was a T in the pipe.

My image of it when the Becks had it was of Anna and Bob always looking worn out and always working, day and night, and being totally unable to keep up.
—David Walton

Owning Tassajara was many things. It was marvelous and it was awful sometimes.
—Anna Beck

A great many people went for the baths. The baths were one of the major draws of this particular crowd — what could be called contemporarily "the Marin crowd" — with their hot tubs.

—David Walton

Cartoon by Robert Beck

That era of the Monterey Peninsula was probably one of the highlighted eras because it was, in a sense, the bohemian life—which had always been here—and was not private anymore. They began to spread out. They had places to go and you could meet them there. Suddenly there was la vie bohème *on the Peninsula, and Tassajara was the extension of that.*

—David Walton

Robert and Anna were interested in the arts, literature, music, and international cuisine, and had liberal views about many things, including nudity. This created problems with some of the old-timers who wanted back Helen Quilty's meat and potatoes and the strict routine of the old days. Anna Beck recalled:

> The longer we had Tassajara, the more sophisticated a group we had there. And that sophistication paled on some of the old-timers, who in their own way raised as much hell as anyone could. Some of those guys used to go up there and get absolutely soused — so they didn't swim nude at the Narrows or take communal baths, but in their way they raised just as much hell. Our appeal was to a different caliber of people — to people in the world of the arts — not farmers or growers. In the beginning, we were very concerned that it would be a place just for weekend drunks.

They bought it out of love and a desire to make money out of it, of course. But, with no capital. So they were always fighting the money situation. They were always two steps ahead of the devil.

—David Walton

Dining room, c. 1962

The Becks ran the Springs with a maximum of ten employees. They devised a system for the bar so neither of them would have to stay there bartending all day long. They called it "the honor system." A guest would mix his own drink and mark it down to be included on his bill. The guests were quite fond of this plan.

When Anna and Robert stayed at Tassajara in the winter, they would borrow carrier pigeons from Barry Brothers Feed Store in Monterey. When the telephone and the road were both out they would put a message in a capsule, strap it to the pigeon's leg, and let it go. It would fly back to Barry Brothers and someone would send help.

There were many requests for recipes. In 1965 the Becks published the first *Tassajara Springs Cook Book*.

Anna was a wonderful cook. Every meal was special. —Anonymous

> The food was lousy when the Becks had it. Only people who gave good food were Mrs. Quilty and the Sappoks. For the middle-class people—give them food they like. Not this fancy stuff. They wanted a leg of lamb or a roast beef. The Hudsons and the Becks gave all that French cookin'—put gravy on everything. Italians and Slavonians just wouldn't eat that stuff. —Jack Novcich

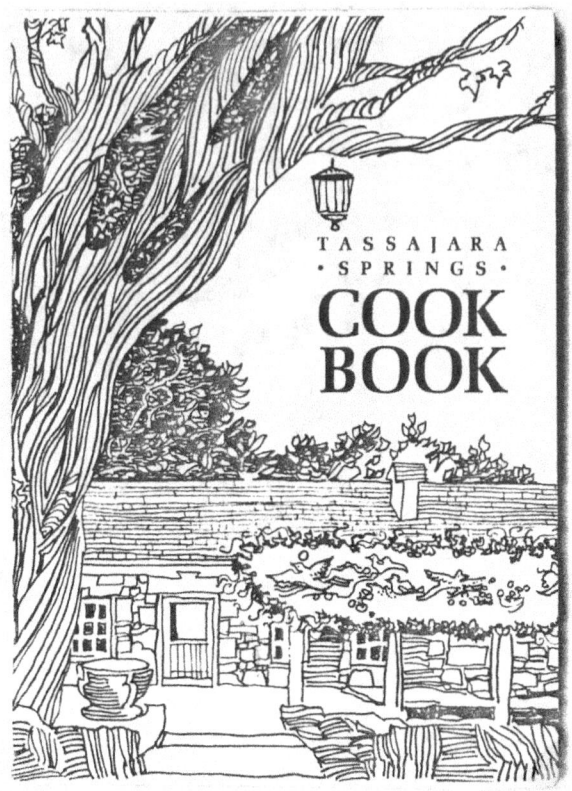

In 1964 Anna Beck gave birth to a son. She ran the Springs during the week and Robert taught school in Monterey and commuted to Tassajara on the weekends. They began to realize Tassajara was more than they could handle, especially with no capital. "One time I figured what we owed and the profit we had made," Robert recalled. "I figured for the time we had put in we'd made 25¢ an hour." They decided to sell the Springs and began to advertise.

Monterey County Retreat

TASSAJARA SPRINGS, remote 160 acre mountain spa, on creek, deep in Los Padres National Forest. County road. Ideal for youth camp, resort, conferences, recreation. For lease or will consider sale to proven conservationist. Write Box 408, Carmel Valley, Calif. Phone 408-372-1480

Wall Street Journal, **December 1964**

By the end of the season in 1965, it was obvious that the choice was either to sell Tassajara or commercialize it. In the summer of 1966 the Becks made one more attempt to keep Tassajara by starting a ten-week craft workshop called Tassajara Encounter. They were given a grant of $5,000 from Ralph K. Davies in San Francisco to get the workshops started. Robert Beck also tried to establish a program he called the Wilderness Trust. The idea of the trust was to have a summer educational art and humanities study center and retreat at the Springs. The Becks hoped to get grants and gifts from foundations and private parties in order to make the program possible. They also wanted to preserve Tassajara as an historical place. Robert remembered:

> We were having fund raisers in San Francisco and making plans to expand the arts and crafts program at Tassajara. We were also negotiating at the same time, with a horseback riders club, to sell the Springs. Anna was getting very tired of having to take over whenever the cook would get drunk, which was often. She was also pregnant with our second child. The Wilderness Trust would have taken tremendous amounts of energy to keep going, and we were still trying to pay off the Hudsons. It seemed like we were physically exhausted and financially bankrupt most of the time.

In late December 1966 the San Francisco Zen Center had just raised enough money for a down payment on the Becks' undeveloped Horse Pasture property. Then the Becks and Zen Center president Richard Baker came to an agreement to apply the money toward the purchase of Tassajara for $300,000. The Becks had planned on selling Tassajara for more, but they really wanted the Zen Center to have it.

TASSAJARA AND ZEN CENTER

SHUNRYU SUZUKI ROSHI, a Zen master from Japan, came to San Francisco in 1959 to fill the position of resident priest of the Sokoji Buddhist Temple on Bush Street. People began to join him in his meditation, and in the early 1960s the group that had formed was incorporated as the Zen Center. Suzuki Roshi wanted a place in the mountains where Zen students could follow traditional practice, including meditation, study, and daily life. After looking at property in several different parts of California, he and his student, Richard Baker, found Tassajara. In early January 1967, with the help of hundreds of supporters, the Zen Center made the first payment toward the purchase of the Hot Springs property from the Becks.

Tassajara Zen Mountain Center gate in snow, c. 1974

The opening day for Tassajara as Zen Mountain Center, Zenshinji (the Zen name) was on July 3rd, 1967. Over 150 people attended. The first training period started the next day. It would be the only one held in the summer, that was two months instead of 90 days, and that allowed students to come for just part of it. It included not only people who had been practicing at the Zen Center, but also some from other groups and teachers. Over 80 people participated in part or whole.

[Roshi, "elder teacher," is often translated as Zen master.]

Students not only practiced Buddhism but also were caretakers of a very old resort. The work involved in maintaining and upgrading the one-hundred-year-old buildings, along with practicing zazen (meditation) from two to six times daily, required real dedication. Tassajara Zen Mountain Center was the first Zen Buddhist monastery and among the first Buddhist monastic communities established in the Western world, and was also the first to have men, women, and couples practicing together. Because nothing quite like this had ever been done before, many aspects of monastic life had to be determined. Whether to wear temple-type robes or American-style clothes? Which ceremonies to adopt? How to arrange living space? Kobun Chino Sensei and Dainin Katagiri Sensei (both of whom would later be called roshi) assisted Suzuki Roshi in helping the new Zen students. A few other priests from Japan came later. The Buddhists also decided to continue having Tassajara open to guests during the summer, which presented its own set of problems. A great deal of time was spent during the first years deciding how the monastery would be organized.

All this took place during the late 1960s, a time when many people in America were looking for a new style of life. Tassajara seemed attractive and different, but just dropping in during the practice periods was not permitted. Wanderers were graciously offered use of the baths and a sack lunch, and were sent back up the road. Drop-ins during the summer could become guest students for a short time if there was room. Those with a genuine interest in studying Zen Buddhism were (and are) encouraged to begin at the City Center in San Francisco, which offers a more formal introduction, with the possibility of returning to Tassajara for practice. No student at Tassajara is exempt from the schedule, and a person has to be serious, because there is no way to live in the situation and not be totally part of it.

From September until May, when there are no guests at the Springs, the Zen students devote themselves to strict monastic life. Practicing at Tassajara is only part of being a student, and some of the students stay several years and then continue their studies in San Francisco, at the Zen Center's Green Gulch Farm in Marin County, at one of the associated centers such as Los Altos or Berkeley, with another group, or on their own. As stated in the Zen Center publication, *Wind Bell*:

> A Zen Monastery is not what "monastery" usually implies in English. It is not a place to retire permanently from the world. A Zen Monastery or meditation center is a place for training, contemplation, and the practice of meditation for a while in a calm and natural environment.

A typical practice period student schedule

3:30 Wake-up Bell	12:00 Lunch
3:45 Han Begins	1:30 Work Meeting
4:00 Zazen	3:15 Tea
4:40 Kinhin	4:00 Docho Roshi Bath
4:50 Zazen	4:30 Student Bath
5:30 Morning Service	5:30 Evening Service
6:00 Breakfast	5:40 Supper
7:10 Study	7:15 Han Begins
8:10 Han Begins	7:30 Zazen
8:25 Zazen / Lecture	8:10 Kinhin
9:35 Work Meeting	8:20 Zazen
11:25 End Work	9:00 Bed
11:50 Noon Service	9:30 Firewatch

han—sounding board hit with mallet, **kinhin**—walking meditation, **docho**—abbot

One of the first projects for the early Zen students was to remodel the old dining room and create a zendo, or meditation hall.

Zendo, c. 1974

The old kitchen had been condemned by the health department when the Becks owned the Springs. It was torn down in the first weeks by an overzealous Zen student caretaker acting on his own who knew it was condemned and thought it looked too dilapidated. The small staff dining shed which already had a four-burner stove was quickly converted into a temporary kitchen. When the hotel burned in 1949, the sandstone blocks were bulldozed into the cellar. Many of these were dug up in the creation of a garden and used as foundation stones for the new kitchen. The walls were made from stones gathered in the creek bed. Roof timbers were cut from Coulter pine from Chew's Ridge and from Tassajara Canyon sycamore. No nails were used in the joints which were made by traditional Danish and Japanese methods. None of the masons had ever built a stone building before. It was finished in 1970.

People didn't want to use the square stones—wanted to use the rounded 'pretty' ones. It took a lot longer, of course. Some people would hunt for the whole day to find the right stone for the right spot. —Paul Discoe, head builder

Kitchen under construction, c. 1970

The baths were replastered and repainted, and the second-story massage rooms, which were in very bad repair, were torn down. A few years later, private sundecks for men and women were built on the roof, but were largely ignored. A carefully crafted, arched bridge provides year-round access to the baths.

Women's side of the baths, 1982

At Tassajara layers of gook melt off and you feel open and tender again.
—Nancy Hockstaff

Bridge to baths, 1982

The old Club House became the new dining room, with the rooms upstairs used as a student dormitory. In 1972 the porch was roofed and screened, doubling the dining capacity. The student diet was lacto-ovo vegetarian with lots of brown rice and vegetables, beans, and fruit, and some eggs and dairy. Until 1970 the guest food included some meat and fish. This diet was difficult for some of the Zen students. Over the years, a vegetarian cuisine has evolved that satisfies the students and the guests, and keeps them healthy. *The Tassajara Bread Book* as well as *Tassajara Cooking* both derived from this cuisine.

Porch on east half of the dining room, 1972

Dining room, 1983

In 1970 Suzuki Roshi, whose health had been poor, recognized his student, Richard Baker, as his successor. Suzuki Roshi died on December 4, 1971. Shortly before his death he installed Richard Baker as chief priest and abbot of Zen Center, and acknowledged him as roshi.

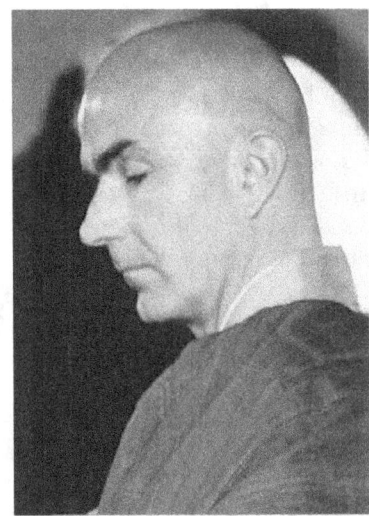

Richard Baker Roshi, c. 1980

Shunryu Suzuki Roshi, 1970

With the winter and spring rains, the road to Tassajara would wash out to some extent every year, some years rendering it impassable for a time until the road crew could get in. Each year it gets a little better. The Monterey County road crew has developed an understanding of the road's contours and watershed requirements; they discovered that if they put dips where the washouts occurred, the water would not collect, but would run off, preventing heavy damage to the road.

Tassajara Road in spring upstream of Jamesburg, c. 1980

At first there were four or five on the crew. By the eighties there were three, with one bulldozer, one motor grader, and one assistant for several weeks in the spring to maintain the fourteen-mile Tassajara Road.

They use'ta have five men with hand rakes who went behind the grader and lifted out the rocks and smoothed the road. —Richard Gomes

In 1973 the Zen Center leased the old Jamesburg house and the snack bar and later purchased the property. It has served as a quite useful halfway house, rest station, place to park the car and go in on the Tassajara stage.

A new building was constructed at Tassajara in 1975. It has six sleeping rooms, all opening on an inner courtyard. Construction incorporated Japanese building techniques, and one of the features was composting toilets at the back of the building.

Had it not been for the Buddhists, Tassajara would probably be some kind of cut-up condominium cabin operation. —H.B. Scott

Courtyard building, 1982

Cabins, 1982

A three-room yurt, built in 1982, was fashioned after the circular, domed tents used by nomadic herdsmen in Siberia. It was built near the swimming pool. The cabins down the lane are much the same as when they were built in the late 1920s.

Yurt building, 1982

Out of the whole year, going to Tassajara is the most special thing I do. I love to go and steam and soak. Forget my life, even if only for a day or two. When I go home I always feel better. —Nancy Hockstaff

Stone bathhouse as guest rooms, 1982

A Brief History of Tassajara

Pine guest rooms, 1982

In August 1977 the Big Sur-Marble Cone fire, which burned 200,000 acres of the Los Padres National Forest, almost destroyed Tassajara.

Laura Burges, a Zen student, remembered, "The Forest Service insisted that we evacuate. It was very strange leaving Tassajara in this long caravan of cars and going up the road and sort of looking back and wondering if we'd ever see it again."

At one point the fire surrounded the monastery. With the aid and guidance of Forest Service Hotshot Crews, backfires were set by Baker Roshi and a few students with fire-fighting training.

In the middle of September, the government brought the Windy Mountain Forest Service Crew from Montana to the Arroyo Seco Forest Station as a mop-up crew. They spent the first two weeks of October in Tassajara Canyon, preparing the area for the winter by removing all fallen wood and brush from the direct line of the stream. The burned watershed created flooding the following winter and spring, and in January 1978, Tassajara Creek went over the top of the steam room and into the plunges; there were landslides in the canyon and the Tassajara Road washed out in six places.

I flew in a helicopter over those mountains after that fire—it was the most desolate burned out landscape I'd ever seen. Probably what Vietnam looked like. —Anonymous

Tassajara Creek, spring flood 1978

In April 1978 the old dining room-zendo burned down. This fire may have started in the basement storage area in a propane gas refrigerator. The wood in the building was so old and dry that it burned rapidly. A new zendo was immediately constructed. The room on the west end of the building was rebuilt in 1982 and is now the office.

Dining room-zendo burning, 1978

We were in there having a ceremony at the end of the training period, and suddenly this voice from the back said, "Hey, there's a fire back here." We all turned around and there's this rosy glow—luckily the door was closed, so it contained the fire long enough for us to all get out. —Laura Burges

Front of the east end, burned dining room-zendo, 1982

A fire in a building as old as that burns so hot and so fast you have very little chance of saving it. —Anonymous

New office on west end of former stone dining room-zendo, 1982

The old hotel stairs lead to the zendo

It is 1985, and the Zen Buddhists have been at Tassajara for eighteen years. Although Tassajara is a monastery, it is also a place where in the summer guests can enjoy the mountains, bathe in the hot springs, or join the Zen students in work or meditation. It is open to guests from May through September. Reservations are required.

It has been one hundred and ten years since Jack Borden advertised that Tassajara Springs was "open to visitors." There have been many changes: fires, floods, new buildings, and new owners; yet Tassajara remains a very special place.

The saying is, "One trip to Tassajara assures you will want to be a yearly visitor as long as you live."

Enso (*sumi* circle) **by Shunryu Suzuki, 1966**
Now the logo of the San Francisco Zen Center

Tassajara Hot Springs, 1983
on the way in past the gate

When we hear the sound of the pine trees on a windy day, perhaps the wind is just blowing, and the pine tree is just standing in the wind. That is all that they are doing. But the people who listen to the wind in the tree will write a poem or will find something unusual. This is, I think, the way everything is.

Shunryu Suzuki

AFTERWORD

MARILYN MCDONALD'S *A Brief History of Tassajara* brings us up to a time thirty-three years ago when the San Francisco Zen Center had been the owner of that beloved place for eighteen years. For almost a century before the Zens, as we were often called, Tassajara had been principally associated with one or two hearty individuals who settled, homesteaded, bought, and ran it. With Zen Center in charge, however, there's been a gradual turnover of resident students and teachers. We have been there for fifty-one years, slowly catching up with the Quiltys, whose reign covered a span of sixty. Now Tassajara's caretaker is a spiritual community, as I envision it had been for millennia before the descendants of Europeans came.

There have been some developments since 1985. The structural integrity of the old bathhouse had gotten a failing grade from our own engineer and so it was rebuilt, and quite nicely, ready for the 1986 guest season. The paint had hardly dried when geological engineers deemed the steep hillside above with a huge looming boulder unstable. So, since 1996 the bridge leads to a roofless ruin and the newer new plunges and steam rooms are upstream a bit on the north side of the creek by the path. The Stone Rooms were redone in the late eighties using the original walls, and a handful of cabins have been replaced. Also still standing are the original stone walls from the zendo that burned down in 1978. It's part of a dining area again, open air, screened in with a roof for student meals in the guest season and work periods. In the late nineties, the charming old dining hall with nine dorm rooms above was rebuilt along with the deck to look and feel much the same, still with hand-hewn logs from the mountain in the ceiling of what once was called the Club House. Tassajara is now almost completely on solar power, including some beautiful solar lamps replacing the old smoky kerosene ones. There's been development just about everywhere, from the entryway, shops, pool area, gardens, landscaping, upper and lower barn, to Grasshopper Flats out beyond the baths.

The Kirk Creek Fire in 1999 threatened Tassajara but didn't get there. The massive Big Basin Fire of 2008, however, did creep in from all sides, and five monks who defied the mandatory evacuation saved the place, as is well recorded in *Fire Monks: Zen Mind Meets Wildfire at the Gates of Tassajara* by Colleen Morton Busch.

In response to a request from me for an update on Tassajara since 1985, Leslie James, appropriately at Jamesburg, wrote:

> One change at Tassajara now is that we offer many retreats. Most people who come have some relationship with, or at least curiosity about, Buddhism or meditation. People still come for the serenity and a rest from their busy lives, but Tassajara is quieter than the old days. The work periods started in 1986 in April and September, when skilled workers and others come to help us maintain Tassajara in the interims between guest season and practice periods. What a blessing.

Much is the same as it was before we came, but since 1967 there is no bar, no alcohol or tobacco sold, though guests are free to bring their own. Prior owners made a noble effort to maintain and run Tassajara so well. None had the budget, or the army of residents and volunteers, or received donations and grants like the Zen Center does. For these new Buddhist caretakers though, the wonderful hot water from the springs is not the focus. Nor is the isolated natural setting, nor the bright stars at night. Zen Buddhist practice is why the residents are there. Fortunately for them and for the guests, that practice includes the springs, the creek, the sky at night, working hard, and taking good care of guests and each other without thinking or talking about it too much.

Marilyn McDonald's friend Rose Martinez brought her ashes to Tassajara. Leslie James wrote:

> Marilyn's memorial was May 25, 2017. Actually there were two, one private with just Rose and me where we scattered some of her ashes down to the creek from the site at the hogback near where Suzuki Roshi's memorial stone is. The other was in the zendo for evening service where the Tassajara students could express, by chanting for her, their appreciation for all the work she did to preserve Tassajara's history—with candles, incense, the *Dai Hi Shin Dharani,* and a picture of Marilyn on the altar that Rose brought. At the end of the service, Rose and I offered incense and then anyone who wanted to could do the same.

Thank you Marilyn. Here's your book. And, as you had imagined, in a form that can be shared beyond the Tassajara office.

David Chadwick
April 19, 2018

photo by Shundo David Haye

Tassajara gatehouse with traditional Japanese design, 2016

Sign at entrance—detail from prior photo

APPENDIX

Esselen Tribe of Monterey County
from www.esselen.com

The Esselen were one of the least numerous groups in California, and are often cited, *incorrectly,* as the first California Indian group to become culturally extinct. This picture of Esselen extinction, although pervasive in the literature, is wrong. Not only did the group not become extinct, there is even recent evidence that some Esselen escaped the missions entirely by retreating to the rugged interior mountains. It now appears that a small group survived into the 1840s before filtering to the ranchos and the outskirts of the growing towns.

Most of the extant data on the Esselen has been gathered into one place, in a new book from Coyote Press. In addition to subjects directly related to the Esselen people, it contains a great deal of information on the natural history of the region.

Breschini, G.S. and T. Haversat (2004)
The Esselen Indians of the Big Sur Country: The Land and the People
Available from **Coyote Press**, Salinas

[Esselen referred to on pp. 1-6, 14, 119, 125, 164.]

Tassajara Springs

A. DOUROND, Proprietor.

This famous health resort is now open for the season. The road has been thoroughly repaired and is in excellent condition.

NEW BATHS,
NEW ROOMS.

And other improvements.

MRS. R. H. LEWIS & DAUGHTER

Have charge of the Hotel, and will spare no pains to promote the comfort and pleasure of guests.

THE TABLES

Will be supplied with the best that can be obtained, including game and fish.

HOW TO GET THERE.

Stage leaves Salinas at 8 a. m. every Saturday, stays over night at Jamesburg and arrives at the Springs Sunday noon. Returning—Leaves Springs Thursday, stays over night at Jamesburg, and arrives in Salinas Friday afternoon.

Salinas Weekly Index, June 1890
[positive version smaller on p. 17]

POLLOCK

THE VIEW ARTIST

SAN JOSE, CALIFORNIA

"POLLOCK Makes Photos Anywhere."

HE WILL PHOTOGRAPH

Your House (interior or exterior), your Horse and Buggy, your Family, or anything you may desire. Views of House and Grounds taken from ELEVATION, showing them to the best possible advantage

INSTANTANEOUS VIEWS

OF ANIMALS A SPECIALTY and satisfaction guaranteed. This means that you can obtain a perfect likeness of anything you value, at small cost, and you will realize how great the privilege when you have lost this opportunity.

VIEWS GIVEN AWAY.

The largest collection of local and foreign views in the city always in stock and each purchaser will get one view FREE. Views all neatly labeled with name of place represented and brief description of same—the only properly labeled views to be found in the city. Among our collection of over 300 different views we name the following:

Views from Yosemite, views from Mt. Hamilton and the great Lick Observatory, Bird's Eye Views from San Jose City Hall and Courthouse, all places of interest in the city, including City Hall, Courthouse, Hotel Vendome, State Normal School, Interior and Exterior views of all the Churches. Also Instantaneous views of Flood in San Jose in winter of '89-'90 (only instantaneous views taken), Instantaneous views of Grand Parades in San Jose on the Tercentenary of St. Aloysius death and many other notable occasions. We have views representing all seasons of the year and which picture the principal attractions of San Jose, Santa Clara County and the State at large in all their beauty. These views are sold at wholesale and retail

I Make Views from 20x24 Down to Postage Stamp Size.

Prices Reasonable.   Satisfaction Guaranteed.

J. T. POLLOCK   64 South River Street, SAN JOSE, CALIF.

N. B.—Having our own conveyance, we are prepared to make Photos in Country at Prices as low as in town.

HURLBERT BROS. & CO., PRINT, SAN JOSE

Pollock's ad
[Went with photo on p. 18.]

**Close-ups of J.T. Pollock's horses and wagon and assistant
Early 1890s**
[See p. 18.]

JOHN MORROW'S LETTER.

He Describes Style at Tassajara Springs, Where the Water Is Warm.

Ed. "Sentinel":—I was very much pleased to receive yesterday three packages of the "Sentinel," the first since I left home two weeks ago. It was like meeting an old friend who could tell me all the news from home. We have spent two weeks here very pleasantly. This is a go-as-you-please summer resort. Every one dresses and deports themselves as suit their fancy. There is no extra and useless dressing by the ladies; the most of them wear calico wrappers and shirt waists. Some wear short skirts, bloomers and leggings like the soldiers. The men mostly wear a colored shirt, a pair of pants and shoes—that's all. And at their moonlight dances, which they often have, gentlemen and ladies dress in the same comfortable style. I have seen well-behaved young gentlemen dancing while wearing a red flannel shirt, and without either coat or vest, and they all treat each other with just as much respect, and, in my opinion, as fully as respectable as though the ladies were dressed in silks and satins, with low necked dresses and the men with claw hammer coats and whisky.

Many of the people here are wealthy, and financially able to dress as they please, and that is just exactly what they do. Some come here for an outing, but the majority have some ailment and come for the hot baths and to drink of some of the various kinds of mineral water and for change of climate. The springs are nearly all hot, and one in particular is boiling hot. The springs are numerous and of many different ingredients, among which are sulphur, magnesia, arsenic and many others. They vary in temperature from ice cold to 145 degrees. The baths are sulphur water, the temperature about 106 degrees. Some of the guests here told me that they went into the plunge bath four or five times each day. It is a wonder they are not cooked clear through, bleached, parboiled and wrinkled like a washer-woman's fingers after a hard day's work over a washtub; but any one can bathe as often and as long as they please. It is all the same price, so the oftener you bathe the deeper you go in and the hotter you get, the more you get the worth of your money, even if it should kill you in the attempt.

The climate here is warm and dry, the nights and mornings are what the ladies would call lovely. I can sit out of doors all the evening without a coat. The thermometer in the middle of the day has registered from 80 to 90; yesterday was the hottest. It showed 92 in the shade.

The moonlight here is grander and more beautiful than any place I have ever been. It has a more yellowish, golden color, and when it gilds the tops of these rugged mountain peaks and slowly creeps down their rock-ribbed sides and casts its golden mellow light over all the valley and among the trees, it is indeed grand, and far beyond my power to appreciate or describe.

I do not intend to talk about myself, but I wish to say that all my wife and myself ever want for breakfast is a cup of coffee and some bread and butter or a biscuit. So one morning I had an opportunity to notice, and did notice, the breakfast of one of those invalids who come here for his health and stop at the hotel, and I am of the opinion that he will return home a sound and healthy man. He ordered mush, then ham and eggs, hot buns, hot biscuit and coffee. After disposing of all this he ordered the waiter to bring him hot cakes for two, one man to eat 'em. And this, I suppose, is the effect of five hot baths each day for three weeks; temperature of water 108, depth 4 feet 6 inches. It's wonderful, isn't it?

We have had a good mess of trout several times. Some of the young men go either up or down the creek and always bring home 75 or 80 very good-sized trout, and they are generous enough to give us all we want. The creek is full of large rocks and boulders, and is rather rough fishing ground. In fact, the whole country around here is nearly as rocky as Alpine county, where I traveled last summer.

I leave here tomorrow for Salinas, San Juan, Hollister, San Jose and other places. When I write the word me, I mean my wife, myself and Dolly horse. Our work is about equally divided while on our trips. My wife is boss of the commissary department. I am chief quartermaster, while Dolly horse is superintendent of locomotion and transportation, and we all attend to our duties faithfully and successfully.
JOHN MORROW.

Tassajara Springs, Aug 3d.

John Morrow letter, 1901
[See pp. 40-42 for two other letters and photo of Morrow.
See www.cuke.com/tass-marilyn for easier reading.]

July 14 1904 Thurs

Surveyed to a pt about ½ mile up Tassajara Cr above mouth of Willow Cr.

July 15 Fri

Moved camp to Tassajara Cr about 2 miles below springs. Surveyed to camp at noon P.M. Fished.

July 16 Sat

Paul Parker, Ai Abbott and myself all knocked out with diarrhoea presumably from polluted water from sewage & offal at Tassajara Spgs. We walked to Spgs had lunch and carried survey from Spgs down to lower narrows in P.M.

July 17 Sun

Surveyed from narrows to end of our line at camp. Finished survey at 10 A.M. Pete, Paul, & I went to Tassajara

Field Notes from
Lou G. Hare, Monterey County Surveyor
Tassajara-Piney Creek Survey, 1904

Cockrill and Abbotts packed outfit to Abbotts where we left our wagon. Cockrill to drive wagon and outfit to Salinas.

We 3 lb loaf at 6 pgs and while rest up. Bath

July 18 Mon Tassajara Spgs
Loafed & bath.

June 19 Tues "
Loafed & bath. Krough & Parker started on foot for Salinas.

July 20 Wed "
Went over survey with Meiners Wm Jeffry and Carr Abbott
Eve when we returned to Spgs learned one of the guests Joe Daga blacksmith from San Jose had shot himself accidentaly with rifle.

July 21 Thurs
I intended to go to Salinas Saturday but as there will be a full stage that day and only 3 others going in today I decided to go today.

July 3 Sun 1904
Accounts.
1 PM Base ball game
July 4 Mon 1904
Celebrated.
July 5 Tues
Getting ready for Arroyo Seco Road Survey.
July 6 Wed 1904
Started on Arroyo Seco Survey Trip. Took Pete Krough and Paul Parker. 4 horses & spg wagon. Ed Littlefield drove. Left Salinas about 8 AM Ar Soledad 11 AM Lunch. Lv Soledad 1 PM Ar Ai Abbotts 7 PM, camped about ¼ mile above Abbotts.
Jul 7 Thurs
Littlefield returned to Salinas with the leaders.
Loafed.

Jul 8 Fri 04
Began work at Piney P.O.
surveyed up present road.
Fred Cockrill joined us this eve. will cook

Jul 9 Sat
Brought survey up to Camp.
Eve went swimming

Jul 10 Sun
Fred Cockrill aug & I on horse back
looked over line as far as Leigh's
Adobe. PM we connected
Survey with S.E. cor T 19 – S
Engaged Ai Abbott & his son "John" to
chop brush.

Jul 10 Mon.
Carried survey to below "Pools"

Jul 12 Tues
Moved Camp to Leigh's Adobe.
Hired 2 pack horses from Abbott.
Carried Survey to "Dam site".

Jul 13 Wed
Carried survey to Leigh's Adobe

[These notes referred to p. 43.
Earlier surveys referred to pp. 6-7.]

Appendix

From records of
Monterey County Road Department, Salinas

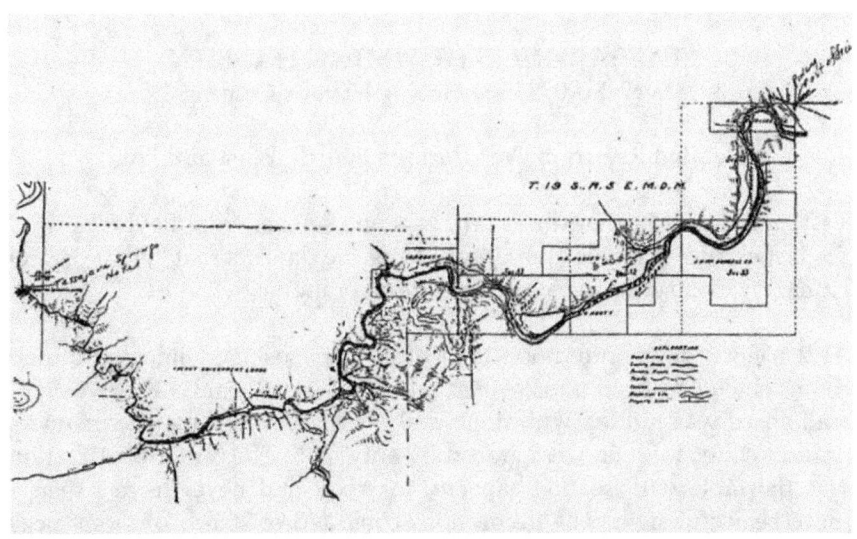

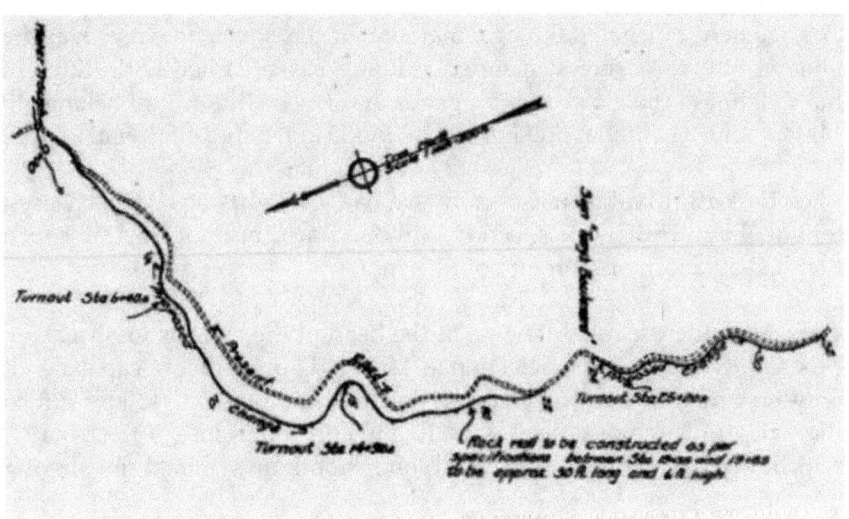

[See p. 56 for another Road Dept. record.
See enlarged versions at www.cuke.com/tass-marilyn.]

From the *Salinas Daily Index,* July 16, 1914
[transcription of article on p. 67]

TASSAJARA IS HUMMING HAPPILY
Everybody There Gets All That's Coming

Belated Report of the Glorious Fourth, Feast and Fun

Tassajara, July 15.—Fourth of July was one scream from daybreak until the last strains of music at midnight bade the dancers that "Home Sweet Home" was the grand finale of a great celebration.

At 2 o'clock in the afternoon the guests were ushered into the dining room which had been transformed into a bower of beauty. Every inch of wall space was hidden with huge brake ferns through which streamers of red, white and blue were gracefully entwined. The center of attraction was the table with seating capacity for sixty and never have I seen a more beautiful sight. The decorations consisted of stands of sweet peas of the national colors while a beautiful center piece was a skillful arrangement of small silk flags, maidenhair ferns and flowers. Over the table at intervals were suspended hanging baskets filled with different hued dahlias. The effect was gorgeous and the credit of it all belongs to Messrs. Chas. L. Pioda, Bob Ford, Paul Pioda and Sergeant Scheu.

Then the eats! My; but what a time we had—all sorts of salads, cheeses, tongue, ham, fruits, cakes, candy, nuts and last, but not least, a punch that had an enormous amount of kick in it.

Chas. L. Pioda occupied the seat at the head of the table as toast-master. Mrs. Quilty made a wise selection as Mr. Pioda proved very capable, not only making a fine address himself but inducing others to follow suit so that wit and laughter flowed with the punch. At the close of the banquet which occupied two hours, everyone stood and joined in singing "America."

At 5 o'clock the races took place—potato, egg, sack, and three-legged, and much amusement was afforded. Little Bill and Jim Jeffery entered in nearly every contest and won first money many times.

Last week we had a mock divorce trial that caused great fun. Mr. Pioda was the all-just and all-wise judge, and after hearing the testimony of many witnesses and arguments of the able counsel—Professor D.C. Ahlers of Santa Cruz and Sergeant Otto Scheu, U.S.A., the verdict was the parties be condemned to live together in perfect connubial bliss for the rest of their lives.

Today there was a great barbecue. Tables were set under famous old Gossip Oak, and steaks broiled to perfection by Dan Leddy of Watsonville and Pete Wallace of Salinas. Bob Ford made the salad and helped in every capacity at once, so you know how "quiet" things were. Fifty-four were seated and about half through eating when an automobile arrived with five guests. A few minutes afterward two wagon loads of campers added to the crowd, and three government men came in on horseback, but there was plenty to eat for all. There are three by Mr. Wm. Hatton of Monterey, one by Bill Rhyner of Spreckels and one by Jim Oksen of Watsonville. Deer was very plentiful this year everywhere.

Mr. and Mrs. Chas. Bardin arrived Friday.

Mutt is one of the principal card games and at any time a game is easy to get.

The weather is very delightful this year, being neither hot nor cold. Will send another budget soon.

MESCAL

A Brief History of Tassajara

Postcards
[color versions at www.cuke.com/tass-marilyn]

Hotel, c. 1900

Pool below the Narrows

Appendix

More ads by the Becks
[as seen on p. 123]

Tassajara springs

AN OUT OF THE WAY RESORT IN THE MOUNTAINS BETWEEN CARMEL VALLEY AND BIG SUR

So far this year Tassajara has had 181 days free of fog. Probably there will be more.

In addition to no fog, we can offer swimming, strolling, angling, horseshoes and other gentle recreations — not to mention our venerable hot mineral plunges and vapors. The food and drink is unusually good.

It's likely the vacation spot you've been looking for.

Write—Tassajara Springs, P.O. Box 68
Carmel Valley, California

Phone—Tassajara Springs No. 1

Tassajara springs — No Summer Fog In Eighty Years

TASSAJARA SPRINGS

A VERY OLD AND REMOTE SPA IN THE SANTA LUCIA MOUNTAINS BETWEEN CARMEL VALLEY AND BIG SUR

Tassajara began business as a resort in 1880. Its character has not changed a great deal since that time.* It offers a comfortable retreat into a vast and spectacular wilderness area, imaginative food and drink, bathing, swimming, sunshine and serenity. Available also are other recreations as gentle as croquet or strenuous as hunting the Russian wild boar. It's a wonderful place to unwind.

Write Box 68, Carmel Valley   Phone Tassajara No. 1

*Even the road is in somewhat original condition and occasionally provides a nice test for motor and motorist.

A Brief History of Tassajara

THE TASSAJARA HOT SPRINGS LEGEND
[from the bathhouse mural, p. 119]

There once was an Indian chief, who was all powerful. He was the favorite of the Sun God that ruled the universe and from this deity received his powers. So supernatural was he that he could hear the grass grow and see his enemies and game a day's travel away. The chief had a young sister who was very dear to his heart and when she became stricken with a strange malady, the hills and dales were ransacked for herbs by the medicine man for a cure. Everything failing, the brother started her on a trip to the big water, hoping that the ocean would help her. By the time Tassajara Creek was reached the sister had failed so much that she could not go further. All powers of the chief had failed and her life was ebbing slowly. Finally in desperation he prayed to his Sun God, offering his own body as a sacrifice. He fell prone on the ground. Although it was mid-day the sun was soon obscured and the earth became dark. The body of the chief stiffened and he grew ridged and was turned to stone. As he dissolved into a mass of rock, hot tears poured forth. The sister fell prostrate over the sacrifice, and was soon covered with hot tears of her sorrowing brother. When she rose she was completely cured. The news of the miracle spread among the Indian tribes of California, and every year the lame, the halt and the blind wend their weary way to bathe in the hot waters which poured from the rock where the chief had died.

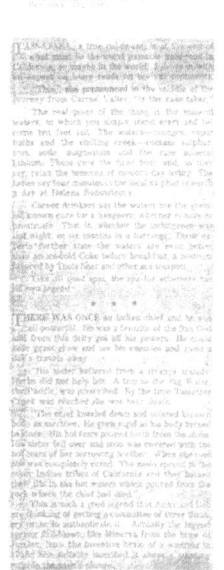

[See pp. 118-119 for more on the Indian legend and p. 124 for a transcript of the article on it by Charles McCabe. Contrary to what McCabe wrote, Annemarie Brunken got the legend from a poem. Some Esselen descendants who've seen the painting and legend report that while the garb and teepee are not accurate, the legend is reminiscent of what their grandparents had told them. The paintings and legend on pp. 71-72 are unrelated and made up at the time. For more see www.cuke.com/tass-marilyn.]

San Francisco Chronicle,
October 31, 1962

Appendix

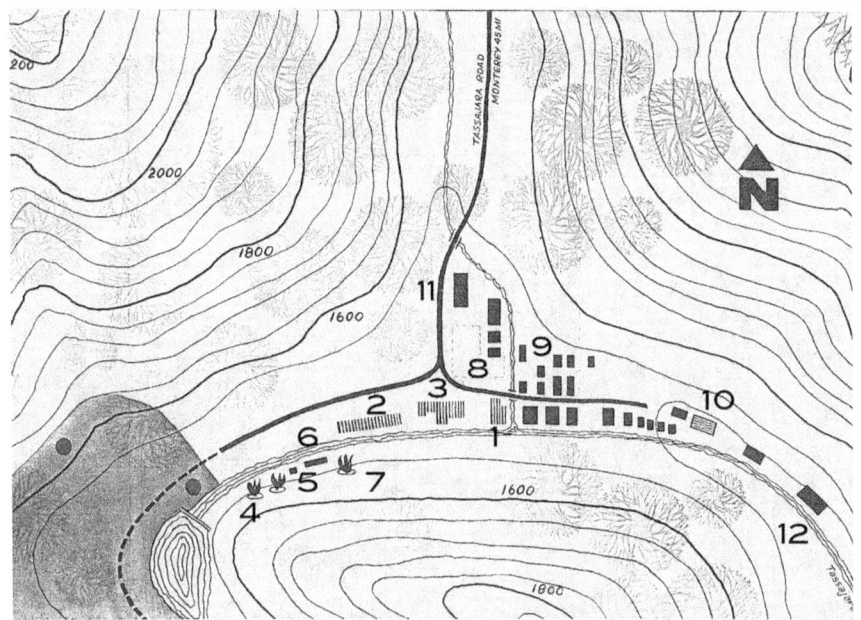

Map of Tassajara Hot Springs

1. Early club house, 1983 dining room
2. Stone bath house, 1983 guest rooms
3. Early dining room, 1983 office and zendo ruins
4. Hot springs
5. Plunges
6. Steam room
7. Magnesium spring
8. Hotel location, 1983 zendo
9. Cabins
10. Swimming pool
11. Early bowling alley
12. Barn

Notes on Map
  Upper barn between 10 and 12
  The Narrows downstream SE off map to the right
  Flag Rock NE upper right corner
  Grasshopper Flats roughly the dark area bottom left
  Hogback above Grasshopper Flats

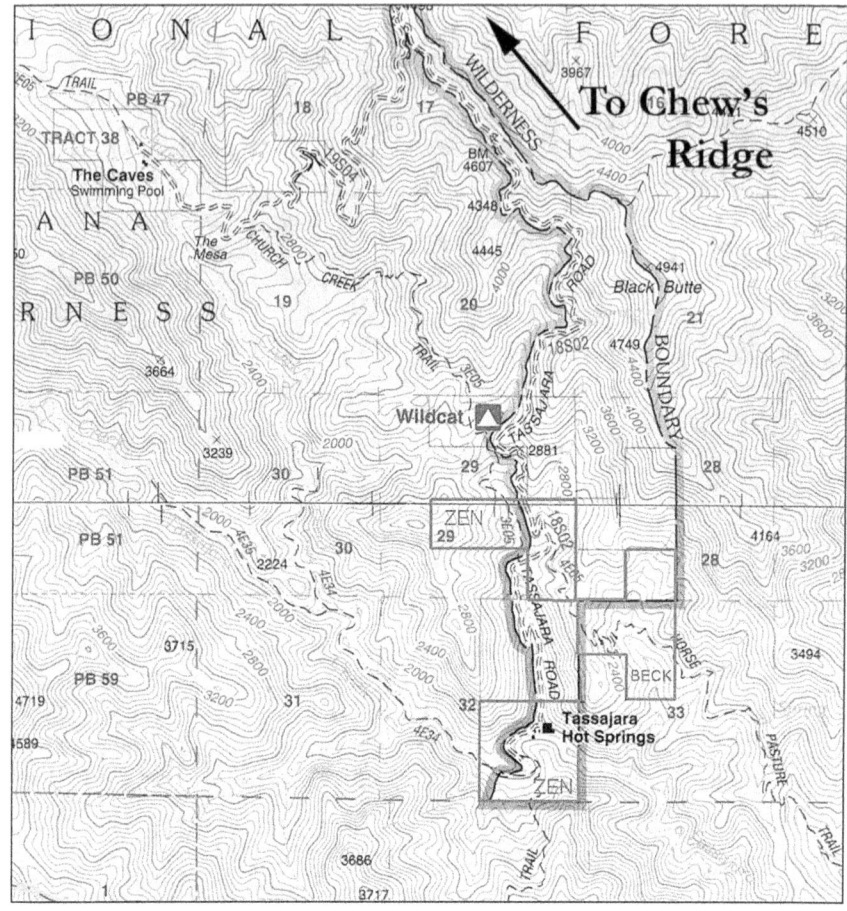

The Tassajara 160-acre parcel and the 160-acre piece to the north are owned by San Francisco Zen Center. The 160-acre Beck parcel (aka Horse Pasture) was purchased by Wilderness Land Trust and transferred to U.S. Forest Service, Monterey District, Los Padres National Forest. The 160-acre Beck parcel is now part of the Ventana Wilderness. "The Caves" private parcel (aka Church Ranch) and the 120-acre piece immediately to the east are owned by the Taylor family of Salinas. (Nikki Nedeff and Ventana Wilderness Alliance, 2018.)

Appendix

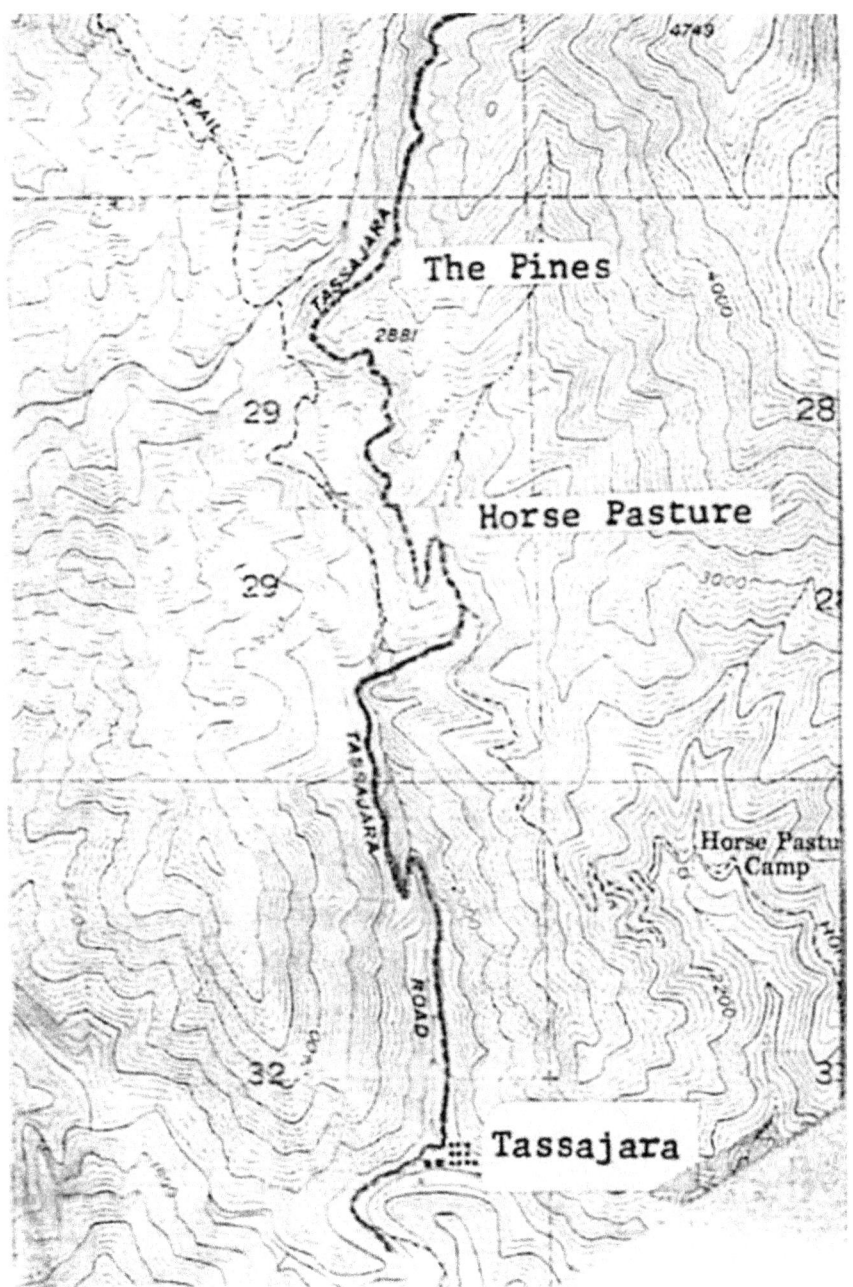

Closeup map of Tassajara/Pines/Horse Pasture area

Temperature	59° C. (138° F.)
Properties of reaction:	
Primary salinity	63
Secondary salinity	0
Tertiary salinity	0
Primary alkalinity	30
Secondary alkalinity	7
Tertiary alkalinity	138

Constituents.	By weight.	Reacting values.
Sodium (Na)	81	3.51
Potassium (K)	4.6	.12
Calcium (Ca)	5.3	.27
Magnesium (Mg)	Trace.	Trace.
Iron (Fe)	1.5	.05
Aluminum (Al)		
Sulphate (SO_4)	110	2.29
Chloride (Cl)	6.5	.18
Carbonate (CO_3)	41	1.37
Arsenate (AsO_4)		
Silica (SiO_2)	118	3.90
	367.9	
Carbon dioxide (CO_2)	0	.00
Hydrogen sulphide (H_2S)	25	1.49

Water analysis of Tassajara Hot Springs, in *Springs of California* by Gerald A. Waring. Government Printing Office, 1915
Analysis by F.M. Eaton, 1909
Constituents are in parts per million.

Appendix

Temperature	58.5
pH	9.31
Silica (SiO2)	110.
Sodium (Na)	82.
Potassium (K)	2.5
Calcium (CA)	2.2
Magnesium (Mg)	<.05
Lithium (Li)	.02
Rubidium (Rb)	.02
Cesium (Cs)	<.1
Ammonium (as N)	<.1
Iron (Fe)	<.02
Manganese (Mn)	<.005
Mercury (Hg)	.007
Bicarbonate (HCO3)	102
Carbonate (CO3)	12
Sulfate (SO4)	52
Chloride (Cl)	1.
Fluoride (F)	5.4
Boron (B)	.25
Sulfides (as H2S)	16.
Gas Sample Analysis (vol)	
Nitrogen (N)	96.83
Oxygen (O2)	.04
Argon (A)	1.39
Carbon Dioxide (CO2)	<.01
Methane (Ch4)	1.46
Ethane (C2H6)	<.05
Hydrogen (H2)	<.01
Helium (He)	<.02
Total	99.72

**1977 analysis of water from Tassajara main hot spring
Concentrations are in milligrams per liter.
Source: U.S. Geological Survey**

ACKNOWLEDGEMENTS

I WANT TO THANK everyone who invited me into their homes and gave me photographs, albums, lists of folks to interview, glasses of wine, and cups of tea—not to mention all the memories they shared so freely. I have special warm thoughts of Ira Bailey and Irma Reaves. They both became my friends. The time I spent with all these people and at the Springs is a high point in my life. What an experience—to learn about Tassajara from the people who loved it. The staff at the Monterey County Historical Society were always helpful, as were clerks in the Salinas City offices, the Roads Department, the John Steinbeck Library, Monterey Library, and the Harrison Library in Carmel.

Marilyn McDonald

ON PRODUCING THIS BOOK

THIS BOOK was originally put together as a scrapbook. Pages were added with text typed around photos taped to the pages. The material was saved in a three-ring binder at Tassajara Zen Mountain Center. This was in the 1980s before easy availability of digital files.

Mark Stromberg, Resident Director of the Frances Simes Hastings Natural History Reservation of University of California Berkeley in nearby Carmel Valley, was a friend of Marilyn McDonald interested in seeing her research preserved. He scanned the pages in 2011 with Marilyn, who was by then living in Santa Fe, New Mexico. The scans were combined into a PDF file.

In August 2017 the text from this file was transcribed in Indonesia by Alice Dill Wedland, with help from David Chadwick. The transcription was edited by Marilyn's son, Lawrence Burns, in January 2018. That same month, Mark Stromberg optimized each scanned image and combined them with the digital text file into six by nine inch book form. The manuscript was further edited and developed by Peter Ford and David Chadwick with Lawrence Burns' oversight as a Cuke Archives project. Andrew Main expertly copy-edited and assisted with design and production. David's wife, Katrinka McKay, Paul Spier, Arnie Kotler, and Michael Katz provided valuable suggestions. In Indonesia, Ketut Sastrawan and Jonathan Latupeirissa gave indispensable technical assistance. For the second printing, Jamie Avera of Texas Photo Restoration adjusted eleven images.

Mark Stromberg and Marilyn McDonald were able to archive all background materials, original photos, brochures, clippings, etc. at the Bancroft Library, University of California Berkeley. These materials can be found there under the name of Marilyn McDonald.

For further information on Tassajara history, this book, and Marilyn McDonald, go to www.cuke.com/tass-marilyn.

photo c. 1985 by Bill Bowman

Marilyn McDonald
November 26, 1940–January 3, 2017

INDEX

Abbott House, 15
Abbott, Ai (?), 155, 157-158
Abbott, Carr, 21-22, 41, 156, 158
Abbott, John, 158
Ahlers, D.C., 67, 161
Anthony, J.C., 49
Arnold, Henry Wallace, 34
Arnold, Henry, 19-20, 34-35
Arnold, Robert, 15, 19-20
Arroyo Seco Creek, 3, 34, 40, 41, 44, 52, 99, 140
Bailey, Ira, 16-17, 22, 31, 51-54, 57, 62, 71, 73, 82-85, 90, 170
Baker, Richard, ix, 129, 131, 137, 140
Bardin, Mr. & Mrs. Chas., 67, 161
Barkdull, Walter, 106-107
Barry Brothers Feed Store, 127
Bears, viii, 5-6
Beasley, Rocky, 5
Beck, Anna, 87, 121-129, 131, 134, 163, 166
Beck, Robert, 44, 120-129, 131, 134, 163, 166
Berkeley, 132
Big Sur, 140, 149, 163
Blaine, A.T., 10
Boling, Leon, 7
Borden, Jack B., 8-9, 143
Branagh, George, 106
Breschini, G.S., 149
Brewer, William, 5
Bruce, 34
Brunken, Annemarie, 118, 164
Bundgard, James, 99
Burges, Laura, 140-141
Cachagua, 5, 32
Cahoon, Mae, 24
Canfield, Dr., 44
Carmel Valley, 4, 15, 32, 40, 44, 123, 124, 128, 163, 171
Carmel, 3, 32, 41, 83, 120, 170
Cascades, 54, 85
Castroville, 43, 115
Chew, 32
Chew's Ridge, 5, 13-14, 134, 166

China Camp, xi, 3, 13-14, 17, 94
Chinese, 13, 19, 63, 81
Chino, Kobun, 132
Church, Sarah, 34
Churches (family, creek, caves & ranch), 1-5, 18, 166
Clark, Henry, 51
Clinefelter, Paul, 31, 49, 64, 73, 89, 96
Cockrill, Charles, 63
Cockrill, Fred, 156-158
Cornett, I.J., 88
Cozzeres, H.F., 56
Crawford, Joan, 106
Crowe, Mr. & Mrs., 40
Curran, Jack, 106
Daga, Joe, 37
Davies, Ralph K., 129
Del Monte, Hotel, 52
Discoe, Paul, 134
Doctorow, E.L., 66
Dourond, Anthony, 13, 17, 150
Duda, Al, 83
Eaton, F.M., 168
Elliot, Mrs., 9
Enevoldsen, Ella, 39, 45-46, 61, 74
Ernst, Pop, 52
Faul, Elmer & Sybil, 101
Fisher, Harrison, 72
Flag Rock, 74-75, 96, 165
Ford, Bob, 67, 161
Foster, Billionaire, 47
Foster, William "Pat", 87
Franco Hotel, 115
G.A.R. (Grand Army of the Republic), 38
Gilroy, 36
Gomes, Richard, 138
Gonzales, xi
Gossip Oak, 62, 66-68, 70-71, 103, 113, 161
Granger, Mrs. Jefferey, 40
Grasshopper Flats, the Flats, 61, 86, 145, 165
Greenfield, xi

Hagan, James, 11
Hall, John D., 7
Hallock, Mr., 16, 79
Handley, William, 62
Hansen, G.P., 63
Hare, Lou G., 43, 155-158
Harkins, Mary, 72
Harlan, J.W., 5
Hart, William, 9-11, 63
Hatton, William, 67, 161
Haversat, T., 149
Hawley, Elita, 58
Hill, W.J., 15
Hillsboro, 107
Hockstaff, Nancy, 135, 139
Holohan, James, 92, 98
Horse Pasture, 48, 63, 129, 166-167
Howell, Dorthea, 123
Hudson, Lester & Margaret, 120-121, 123, 127, 129
Hudson, Tom & Jane, 120-121
Hughes, Mrs., 122
Indian Legends (faux), 71-72, 118-119, 125, 164
Indians, Esselen & others, viii, 1-6, 14, 34, 119, 125, 129, 149, 164
James and Chew, 32
James, John (& Ranch), 9, 12-13, 16, 32-33
Jamesburg, viii, 3, 5, 15, 17, 19, 32-35, 37, 40, 54, 87, 94, 123, 137-38, 146, 150
Jeffery House (Hotel), 15, 21-22, 57, 94
Jeffery, Bill, 37-38, 42, 50-53, 74, 156
Jeffery, Charles William, 11, 72
Jeffery, Little Bill & Jim, 67, 160
Jim, Sunny, 79
Juhler, Mrs., 47
Katagiri, Dainin, 132
Kent, Mr., 32
King City, 106
Kingsbury, George & Mrs., 88
Knough, Peter, 155, 157-158
Koue, Harry, 39, 59, 61, 82
Kraul, Svend, 93
Kroeber, A.L., 2
Laird, Irene, 92, 94
Laird, Malcolm, 92-93
Lamb, Richard, 87, 118

Lambert, Bill, 49, 73, 86-87, 94, 98, 101, 123
Laureles Grade, 15
Leddy, Dan, 67, 161
Leibbrandt, Mr., 40
Leigh, J.W., 10
Levitt, Julie, 117
Lewis, Charles, 40
Lewis, Mr. (& ranch), 15, 40
Lewis, Mrs. R.E. & daughter, 17, 150
Lilienthaln, Philip, 107
Littlefield, Ed, 157
Logwood, Joe, 5-6
Los Altos, 132
Los Lauralis (ranch), 40
Los Padres National Forest, xii, 98, 112, 128, 140, 166
Lumpy, Little Bum, 118, 123
Machado, Chris, 88
MacLean, Mrs., 47
Marin County, 132
McCabe, Charles, 124-125, 164
McGregor, Laura, 30
McKinney, John B., 53
McPhail, Grace (Dodge), 63
McPhail, J.R., 13
McPhail, Wilburn, 63
Mehne, R.E., 103, 107-108, 110
Menasco, Mrs., 59
Mescal (pen name), 67, 161
Monterey Co. Board of Supervisors, 8, 18, 35, 42, 57
Monterey Co. Road Dept, 43, 159, 170
Monterey, xii, 3, 6, 8, 32, 40, 43, 44, 95, 107, 118, 124, 161
Morrow, John, 40-42, 154
Myers, Helen (Myers-Terry), 99, 101-103, 105-108, 110, 112, 114
Myers, Ralph, 99-101
Myers' kids, Edwin, Mary, Michael 105, 107, 112
Narrows, The, 12, 76, 126, 162, 165
New York, 99, 112, 124
Novcich, Jack, vii, xi, 56, 116, 127
O'Hara, Tom, 21, 54
Oksen, James, Emma & Irma, 36, 67, 161
Oregon, 4, 6, 52
Overholt, Miles, 90
Pacific Grove, 32-33, 38

Index

Pacific Improvement Company, 32
Parker, Paul, 155, 157-158
Pete, 88
Pines, The, 63, 167
Piney Creek, 43, 155-158
Pioda, Chas. L., 67, 160-161
Pioda, Paul, 58, 63, 75-76, 79, 81, 86, 160
Plotnekoff, Doc, 81
Plump, Bert, 107
Pollock, J.T., 18, 151-153
Prader, Phillip, 101
Quilty kids (1st 7), Alice, Estelle, Gertrude, Irene, Mary, Pauline, Ruth, 12, 36-37
Quilty, Charles, 11-13, 15, 18-19, 22, 25, 27, 34-37, 42, 48-49, 63, 99, 145
Quilty, Genevieve, 36-37
Quilty, Helen (Holohan), 31, 36-37, 42, 45, 48-50, 52, 57, 59, 63-64, 66-67, 71-74, 76-77, 81-84, 86, 88, 92, 96, 98-99, 108-109, 126-127, 145, 160
Quilty, Mary (Jeffery), 12, 36-38, 42
Quilty, Mary, 11-12, 19, 34, 36, 145
Reaves, Irma, 16, 34, 170
Resetar Hotel, 98
Rhyner, Rose, 59, 78
Rhyner, W.J., 67, 78, 161
Robb, Bruce W., 83, 93-94
Roberts, J.L.D., 56
Ronson, Charles, 107
Roscoe, Frederick & Nancy, 121
Ross, Leo, 107
Rossi, Emil, 20
Rust, J.E., 8
Ryans, The, 36
Salinas, viii, xii, 3, 10, 11, 15, 17, 20, 22, 32, 37, 38, 39, 40, 42, 43, 44, 50, 53, 57, 83, 88, 93-95, 99, 106, 154, 170
Sam the Cook, 63-64, 74
San Carlos, 32
San Francisco, 7, 13, 36, 81, 87, 99, 121, 129, 131-132, 143, 145, 166
San Jose, 11-13, 19, 36, 81, 151, 154
San Mateo, 101
San Quentin, 92, 98
Sanborn, Miss, 37
Santa Barbara, 47
Santa Cruz, xi, 40, 92, 161
Santa Lucia Mountains, xii, 1, 6, 18, 32, 44, 79, 81, 106, 118, 163
Sappok, Angela, 115-116, 120, 123, 127
Sappok, Dorothea, 118
Sappok, Frank, 115-116, 118, 120, 127
Sappok, Hans, 115
Scherrer, Helen, 71
Scheu, Sergeant, 67, 160-161
Scott, H.B., 138
Shankle, Mrs., 116
Smithsonian Institute, 44
Stephan's Ranch House & Hotel, 32
Suzuki, Shunryu, vii, ix, 131-132, 137, 143-144, 146
Swan, Jack, 4
Tassajara Bread Book, 136
Tassajara Cooking, 136
Tassajara Hot Springs Co., 88
Tassajara Springs Cook Book, 127, 128
Taylor family, 166
Terry, Phillip, 103, 105-107, 112
Tharp, Loly & Joseph, 63
Tony Trail, 10
Tony's Boulevard, 54, 57, 83
Tularcitos, 32
U.S. Forest Service, 106, 107, 140, 166
Vanderhurst, Kenneth, 83
Ventana Wilderness Alliance, 166
Victorine, Lilian, 79
Wallace, Pete, 67, 161
Walton, David, 122, 125-126
Waring, Gerald A., 168
Watsonville, 36, 37, 39, 40, 43, 61, 77, 81, 95, 98, 107, 161
Westphal, Richard, 47
Whalen, Mamie, 61
Whitlocks, 15
Wilderness Land Trust, 166
Wilderness Trust, 129
Williamson, Oliver, 2
Willow Creek, 3
Wind Bell, 132
Yardell, Mrs., 122

www.ingramcontent.com/pod-product-compliance
Lightning Source LLC
Chambersburg PA
CBHW071201070526
44584CB00019B/2878